YOU

YOUR ROAD MAP TO BECOMING FIERCE, FREE, AND FULL OF FIRE

JEN HATMAKER

NELSON
BOOKS

An Imprint of Thomas Nelson

Glorious You

© 2021 Jen Hatmaker

Published in Nashville, Tennessee, by Nelson Books, an imprint of Thomas Nelson. Nelson Books and Thomas Nelson are registered trademarks of HarperCollins Christian Publishing, Inc.

Published in association with Yates & Yates, www.yates2.com.

Thomas Nelson titles may be purchased in bulk for educational, business, fundraising, or sales promotional use. For information, please e-mail SpecialMarkets@ThomasNelson.com.

Any internet addresses, phone numbers, or company or product information printed in this book are offered as a resource and are not intended in any way to be or to imply an endorsement by Thomas Nelson, nor does Thomas Nelson vouch for the existence, content, or services of these sites, phone numbers, companies, or products beyond the life of this book.

ISBN 978-1-4002-3095-2

Printed in the United States of America

21 22 23 24 25   LSC   10 9 8 7 6 5 4 3 2 1

CONTENTS

Who I Am: I AM WIRED THIS WAY

Who I Am: I AM EXACTLY ENOUGH

Who I Am: I AM STRONG IN MY BODY

CONTENTS

What I Need: I DESERVE GOODNESS

What I Need: I NEED SOME HELP

What I Need: I NEED MORE CONNECTION

CONTENTS

What I Want: I WANT THIS DREAM

What I Want: I WANT TO
CHOOSE MY YESES

What I Believe: I BELIEVE
IN SPIRITUAL CURIOSITY

What I Believe: I BELIEVE IN THIS CAUSE

How I Connect: I WANT TO
CONNECT WITH HONESTY

CONTENTS

How I Connect: I WANT TO
CONNECT WITHOUT DRAMA

FINAL THOUGHT

WELCOME TO FEROCITY, FREEDOM, AND FIRE

When I was a girl, I had a multifaceted vision for my future: librarian, horse rider, or backup dancer for Janet Jackson (I contained multitudes!).

When you were a girl, what was your big dream?

Maybe you imagined that you would grow up to be the next fierce lyrical diva, the likes of Aretha or Cher. Perhaps you saw yourself flying free toward the net, like WNBA legend Sheryl Swoopes. Or maybe you saw yourself delivering fiery rhetoric, like Sojourner Truth or Malala Yousafzai, advocating for justice. When we're young, we dream of who we might become.

And then . . . life.

Along the way, we notice that the Men in Charge are sort of handling all the big jobs. We're coached by well-behaved women to color inside the lines. Follow the rules. Please the Men in Charge. And without ever really planning to, we conform ourselves to the homogenous lady stencil into which we've seen our foremothers squeeze themselves. *(Blech.)*

The roles they've played—chef, wife, mother, house-keeper, caregiver—were important ones. And even ones that might have our names on them! But if we unwittingly repeat what we've seen and known, without pausing to notice if they're for us, we might be lulled into forgetting the dreams that we had when we were young. Dreams that were given to us by God. Somewhere along the way, some of us got lulled into complacency and began to go through the motions expected of us.

But at some point, we look around and we notice women who didn't seem to realize that there was a template at all. It's like they never got the memo about a suffocating pair of lady-Spanx they were expected to squeeze into. And noticing these unlikely women is what began to wake me up.

I watched my mom's best friend, Miss Prissy, be wild when everyone else was proper. That gal made no bones about taking up more space than I'd been taught women were allotted. If Miss Prissy didn't have to apologize for who she was, maybe I could be who I really was.

I was blown away by the first woman I heard preaching the Word from an actual pulpit. Decades of internalized patri-archy were suddenly in jeopardy. And I dared to imagine that if she had something to say, maybe I had something to say.

And . . . Anne Lamott.

That's all.

I mention these marvels because encountering each one

x

transformed me a little bit. To be clear, I didn't necessarily become more like them; I became more like me. Witnessing the glory of someone being who she really is granted me permission to push the envelope a little bit. To posture less. To worry less about the opinions of others. To become more of who I really am.

And this—becoming who one really is—is what I want for you, sister. I want you to roll down the window and throw others' opinions of you right into oncoming traffic. I want you to take off the mask you wear at church, or in prayer group, or in your professional circle and let others see who you really are. I want you to experience the glorious freedom of being exactly the same person on the inside as the person you show the world.

Is it going to disappoint your grandma? Possibly.

When you step outside the box, might those around you feel uncomfortable? Maybe.

Might you feel a little bit like everyone can see your bra strap showing? Likely, yes.

Is it worth it? Absolutely.

You becoming who you really are may ruffle the feathers of those around you who thought they had you pegged. They might not get it. They might think you're just going through a *thing*. But I need you to hear that becoming who you were made to be really isn't about you.

Ummm, Jen, it's kind of exactly about me.

I want to push back on that you-o-centrism. Yes, it's kind of about you. I hear that. But when you step up to be the woman that only you can be, the *world* benefits. Your community benefits. The people on the planet God loves benefit. When you finally decide to shed the costume you thought you were supposed to be wearing and don instead the one-of-a-kind uniform that empowers you to do what only you can do, that's when this party called life really gets good.

In these pages, I'm offering you tools that can help you discern and embrace becoming the woman you were designed to be. Carve out time to spend with this journal and you'll have what you need to know who you are, name what you need, identify what you want, affirm what you believe, and choose how you connect with others.

And at the very end, it's going to be like Christmas morning. Because I'm inviting you to write your own manifesto that both uniquely affirms Glorious You and can also serve as a rudder as you continue to become the Glorious You that the world desperately needs.

You are fierce.

You are free.

You are full of fire.

I am cheering you on in every way, dear sister.

Jen

Who I Am:

I AM WIRED
THIS WAY

Week 1

PAY ATTENTION TO
YOUR LIVED YEARS

You know how our culture has this obnoxious obsession with youthfulness and beauty? Well, if you're committed to this journey of embracing the one and only glorious you, listen up. I've got great news for those who've blown out more than a few birthday candles: our understanding of who we are comes into focus the longer we reside in adulthood. That's a fancy way of saying that when it comes to embracing your fierceness, freedom, and fire, if you are a woman of a certain age, you are *winning*. (At last. Am I right?)

Whether you've lived two-point-five (2.5) decades or seven, the big win here is noticing whether the woman you are on the inside is the same one that the rest of the world is seeing on the outside. If part of you gets tucked away when you're with one squad and is allowed to come out and play when you're with your girls in another crew, I want you to hear that there is a better way to live.

NOODLE ON THIS: What are the particular situations in which you "edit" who you are to accommodate the people you're with?

_____

_____

_____

_____

Noticing the ways you adapt to fit your environment gives you clues that help you identify *who you really are*! As you reflect on your lived years, imagine what parts of yourself you will begin to reveal as you choose to allow the world to see who you really are.

Note and celebrate them here.

_____

_____

_____

_____

Boots on the Ground (Marching Orders)

This week think of that one situation you expect to encounter in which you'll behave differently because you are now choosing to live free. Specifically, how will it look?

_____

_____

_____

_____

_____

_____

_____

_____

_____

_____

_____

_____

_____

This week pay attention to your lived years.

Week 2

NOTICE YOUR PATTERNS

Sometimes discovering the human being you were designed to be does not have to be a big, elaborate mystery. And that's because, to any average bystander or casual observer, there are clues in our lives that are plain as day.

Maybe after your grandma taught you how to make ice cream, you would deliver some to an elderly neighbor every week. Or maybe you started baking birthday cakes when you were twelve and are now catering friends' weddings "on the side." Or you might have been that girl who hustled to sell five hundred boxes of Girl Scout cookies (and the rest of us only hated you a little bit), and now you're making a profit on the small business you started six months ago. (I realize that was just all about food. So sue me.)

NOODLE ON THIS: What do you keep doing? What do you keep saying? How do you consistently respond? What constantly sticks in your craw? What idea do you keep pushing?

What thought do you keep thinking? When does your body tell you how you actually feel? Who do you keep agreeing with? What keeps giving you life? What keeps draining you dry? Where do you keep going, or to whom? What do your instincts and preferences and temperament and gut checks show you?

_____

_____

_____

_____

_____

_____

As you look at those observable patterns in your life, which ones made you feel happy? Which ones pulsed inside you with a surprising energy?

_____

_____

_____

_____

_____

_____

Boots on the Ground (Marching Orders)

This week choose to practice, with your actual body, one of the passions you noticed above. Specifically, how will you live this out?

_____

_____

_____

_____

_____

_____

_____

_____

_____

_____

_____

_____

_____

_____

_____

This week notice your patterns.

Week 3

INVESTIGATE YOUR WIRING

I f you've been quietly thinking that this whole business of discovering the unique snowflake you are feels, well, a little bit self-absorbed, I rebuke you in the mighty name of Jesus. Which I mean in the nicest possible way, of course.

When you do the work to notice and embrace the one glorious you, every human in your orbit benefits: your patient coworkers, your weary spouse, the humans who've come right out of your body or who were birthed in your heart, your dear mother (God love her), and your hairstylist. And also, *you*.

There. That's better. I hope you're happy.

I believe I admitted that I do not naturally self-assess, but when I *have* paused to notice the way I'm naturally wired—*introvert? What?! How am I just discovering this?!*—I've been #blessed.

There are lots of ways to get at this business of identifying the way you're wired, but some of the inventories that have been useful to many include: Myers-Briggs, Strengths Finder, the Enneagram, Jung personality test, the Big Five, and others. (Spoiler alert: be prepared to rejoice in your evident inherent strengths and feel a little defensive about the areas these dumb inventories describe as "weaknesses." Whatever.)

NOODLE ON THIS: From the inventories you've taken in the past, or the one you just googled and found online, what have you learned about your strengths?

_____

_____

_____

_____

_____

And from these recognized personality indicators, what is it they're saying about your weaknesses that you are hearing and are really trying hard to accept?

_____

_____

_____

_____

_____

Boots on the Ground (Marching Orders)

This week consciously purpose to live into one aspect of your natural wiring *in a way that benefits others.* Specifically, how will it look?

_____

_____

_____

_____

_____

_____

_____

_____

_____

_____

_____

_____

_____

_____

This week investigate your wiring.

Week 4

SEEK FEEDBACK FROM YOUR CLOSEST PEOPLE

F or the last few weeks, you've been paying attention to who you are and how you're wired. Kudos to you! On the off chance that your self-assessment could possibly be a teeny weeny bit . . . skewed . . . (true of the general population but doubtfully true of my keenly self-aware readers) I want you to run it past your very closest folks to confirm or deny your findings.

Your email to your best people—*note: you're going to want to blind copy them so there's no chance of them comparing notes and ganging up on you about what actually may be true*—can include a paragraph of what you've discovered from your lived years, about your patterns, and about your unique wiring.

GIVE THIS A WHIRL: Write a paragraph about what you discovered in your first three weeks of self-exploration.

_____

_____

_____

_____

_____

_____

_____

_____

KEEP IT REAL: Return to your paragraph, above, and make sure it includes both your glorious strengths and also your admitted weaknesses and challenges. Note those here.

_____

_____

_____

_____

_____

_____

_____

_____

_____

Boots on the Ground (Marching Orders)

Share your self-assessment with your people and ask, "This is what I said about myself. Is this right? Is this how I am perceived and experienced? Does this feel like an accurate assessment?" Jot down any new insights or surprises here.

_____

_____

_____

_____

_____

_____

_____

_____

_____

_____

_____

_____

This week seek feedback from your closest people.

Who I Am:

I AM EXACTLY
ENOUGH

Week 5

REJECT THE LIE THAT
YOU ARE TOO MUCH

*C*lose your eyes and get in touch with your spunky, badass, six-year-old girl self.

If you've forgotten her, she's the fireball inside you who hadn't yet been bombarded with all the disapproval our culture throws at fierce little girls, insisting they are "too much."

She likely says what she's thinking, without filtering to accommodate her audience.

If she thinks about her physical appearance—which she rarely does because, let's face it, she's got better things to do—she doesn't find fault with it.

She thinks other girls and women are the bomb, and it doesn't occur to her to criticize them or minimize them in any way.

If she was spared early trauma, if she was nurtured and protected, that six-year-old thought she was the bee's knees. The cat's pajamas. The fox's socks. (These are all real things.)

She knew she was exactly enough. If someone had hinted that she was too much, her fierce ears just filtered that mess right out before it reached her brain.

NOODLE ON THIS: Who was the person or people in your life—a relative, a neighbor, a teacher, a coach, a church lady, a friend, the parent of a friend, someone else—who suggested that maybe you were a bit too much?

_____

_____

_____

_____

And as you recall the person or people who communicated that you were too much, what was it about you that seemed to offend them? Was it your wonderfully loud voice? Was it your anti-establishment appearance? Was it your fierce passion? Was it your courage to push boundaries? What was it?

_____

_____

_____

_____

Boots on the Ground (Marching Orders)

This week choose one area in which others deemed that you are "too much," and practice kindness and affirmation toward this authentic part of you. Specifically, how will it look?

_____

_____

_____

_____

_____

_____

_____

_____

_____

_____

_____

_____

_____

_____

This week reject the lie that you are too much.

Week 6

REJECT THE LIE THAT
YOU ARE NOT ENOUGH

Whether you're a black-haired beauty, a ginger, a blonde, or a brunette, you may have seen a hair-lightening product called "Go Blonder." It's genius, really. Because if our society values blondeness (yes, Mattel, with your Barbie doll, we absolutely blame you), even the blondest gals are hood-winked into buying this lightener, reasoning, "Wait? I could be blonder? Here, take all my dollars."

And I have to mention a corollary madness, because it breaks my heart (caution: trigger warning for dark-skinned goddesses): the bazillion-dollar skin-lightening industry is profiting by selling skin-lightening cream to gorgeous black and brown women, as well as already-fair Asian ones, who've breathed the light-skin poison exported by the United States of America.

The lie being rammed down the throats of both the

palest and blondest, as well as the darkest and blackest: that we are not enough.

Sister, *resist*.

NOODLE ON THIS: What are ways in which our culture's insidious lie (did I mention it makes companies bazillions of dollars?) has attempted to convince you that your body, the way you're made, is not enough?

_____

_____

_____

_____

_____

And what are some of the countless other ways that the lie has tried to convince you you're not enough? (Income? Savings? Possession? Education? Career? Other?)

_____

_____

_____

_____

_____

Boots on the Ground (Marching Orders)

This week—and, honestly, all of them—choose one thing about who you are that someone else has deemed "not enough" and embrace it. Specifically this week, how will it look?

_____

_____

_____

_____

_____

_____

_____

_____

_____

_____

_____

_____

_____

This week reject the lie that you are not enough.

Week 7

OWN YOUR MEGA,
MEZZO, OR MODEST

IMHO, one of the most beautiful things in this big world is to see a woman who takes up exactly the right amount of space. And that's what I'm inviting you to notice and affirm in yourself this week.

Mega Women lead and live large. Kamala is one of these queens. She has chosen not to shrink herself to fit the neat and tidy categories some would assign her. (Can we just pause to giggle a little bit about this whole fabulous business of her husband, Doug Emhoff, becoming our country's first "second gentleman"?)

Modest Women have zero interest in taking up all the space that some of these other Mega divas occupy. They don't want it! You might know a woman like this who occupies a humble space and performs small miracles behind the scenes that transform others' lives. They're not loud, but they're mighty.

And Mezzo Women are located somewhere between the Megas and the Modests. But don't for one second think there's anything mediocre about them. No ma'am. These are our bridge builders, peacemakers, compromise brokers, and soothers. Without them, we'd be doomed.

NOODLE ON THIS: Which of these three gals feels most like you, and why?

_____

_____

_____

_____

As you consider your Mega-ness, your Modest-ness, or your Mezzo-ness (really, friend, let's start throwing these around in coffee-time conversations), where have you expressed it and where are you being _invited_ to express it?

_____

_____

_____

_____

_____

Boots on the Ground (Marching Orders)

This week create an opportunity to affirm one other woman for her Mega-ness, her Modest-ness, or her Mezzo-ness. (But before you do, please offer her some context. Without it, each of these sounds like a slam. I hear it.) Specifically, how will it look?

_____

_____

_____

_____

_____

_____

_____

_____

_____

_____

_____

_____

This week own your Mega, Mezzo, or Modest.

Week 8

BE WHO YOU ARE TO FREE
OTHERS TO BE WHO THEY ARE

Here's the thing about women who are comfortable in our own skin: we're contagious. We really are. Have you noticed that? When another woman is being her glorious, genuine self, her authenticity gives others around her permission to be their unique, one-of-a-kind, glorious selves. When an eighty-year-old granny is kicking it at the skate park and you walk by and see her being her badass self, with her li'l ol' white hair poofing out from her helmet, don't you feel like you can be who you really are? I do.

There is some unnamed law of the universe that makes this a real thing. Like, if a woman is taking up the exact amount of space for which she was designed, the other gyno molecules in her orbit naturally tend to react by taking up *their* rightful space. You see how it's science?

When you purpose to be who you really are—not more

and not less—you liberate other women to be who they really are.

NOODLE ON THIS: Who are some of those fiercest women in your world, and in the great big world, who seem comfortable in their own skin?

_____

_____

_____

_____

_____

   And what are the qualities about those fierce, free, fiery women that communicate—to you and to others—that they are being their authentic selves?

What are the cues that signal a woman is being who she is?

_____

_____

_____

_____

_____

Boots on the Ground (Marching Orders)

This week what is one way you will embrace being who you really are? Specifically, how will it look?

_____

_____

_____

_____

_____

_____

_____

_____

_____

_____

_____

_____

_____

_____

_____

This week be who you are to free others to be who they are.

Who I Am:

I AM STRONG
IN MY BODY

Week 9

LOVE YOUR BODY,
DON'T HATE HER

If you had a $25 Target gift card for every time you looked in a mirror and zeroed in on what you perceive to be your physical flaws, how many $25 Target gift cards would you have? Every time you evaluated your thighs. Every time you eyeballed your post-baby belly. Every time you pivoted to check out your naked butt and decided it was either too round or not round enough (#whitegirlproblems). Every time you looked at your glorious one-of-a-kind self and hated your hair. Your nose. Your skin. Your eyelashes. Everything.

Would you ever treat a friend you love the way you treat your body? Wait, I'll answer that. *No.* I have a good feeling about you, and I know you wouldn't treat any one of your girlfriends the way you treat your body (who, for the record, has done literally *nothing else* but serve you your entire life).

If you decided today to love your body, you'd treat her

the way you treat those you love. You'd smile warmly at her. Maybe give her a sassy wink. You might give her a hug. You'd spend time *enjoying* her, walking or cycling or roller skating. And you might even buy her a slice of delicious key lime pie for no reason at all. Beloved, the choice really is yours. Today you can *choose* to love her.

NOODLE ON THIS: When your eyeballs zero in on your physical flaws, where do they land? (This is just for you, so feel free to speak freely.)

_____

_____

_____

_____

(Copy these honest words onto a piece of paper, find a safe place, and set them on fire.)

Now I want you to pivot and make the radical decision, today, to love the body you've been given.

What will you say or do differently because you've made the decision to love her?

_____

_____

_____

_____

_____

Boots on the Ground (Marching Orders)

This week tell a friend that you've decided to love your body and invite her to join you. Together, decide how you will live out love for your bods. Specifically, what will y'all do differently than you are doing right now?

_____

_____

_____

_____

_____

_____

_____

This week love your body, don't hate her.

Week 10

NOTICE HOW YOUR BODY HAS DELIVERED AND THANK HER FOR HER SERVICE

Guess what? For all your decades, advertisers and retailers have been feeding you nonsense, insisting that your abs aren't toned enough, your eyelashes aren't long and thick enough, and your legs aren't sculpted enough. And despite all that malarkey, the fact remains that your body is actually a pretty amazing gal. For all of your days she has housed your character and soul, intelligence and creativity, love and experience, goodness and talents. She's birthed your smartest ideas, your best jokes, and your goofiest expressions. She's spit out your deepest belly laughs, and maybe she's even offered a little celebration tinkle when you couldn't hold all the joy in anymore. Girl, even when she's felt like crap, she has shown up for you and she deserves your gratitude.

For all the shade you throw her way over the years (don't worry, she forgives you), it is now time to say *thank you* to this amazing gal who has not missed even one second of your journey. If you have one of those families that joins hands around the table before the Thanksgiving turkey dinner and says what they're thankful for, you already know how this goes. And don't hold back. I want you to get really effusive about speaking your thanks to this amazing girl.

NOODLE ON THIS: Take a little stroll down memory lane, remembering when you were five and nine and thirteen and nineteen. Some of you badass warriors can even reminisce on thirty-five and forty-nine and sixty-two. (Get it, Queen!) Now notice the amazing things your body was doing at every age to serve you. (Example: Eight, my legs climbed trees like a monkey. Twenty-six, my breasts were making me and my partner happy. Twenty-nine, my breasts were making my baby happy.)

Jot down what your ears, and legs, and lips, and eyes, and arms were up to, and say thanks. (All the parts, really. Even—and maybe especially?—the "unmentionables." Really have fun with those.)

_____

_____

Boots on the Ground (Marching Orders)

This week look in the mirror each morning and say thank you to a different part of your anatomy. Will it feel weird? Absolutely. Will it get easier each day? I believe it will.

_____

_____

_____

_____

_____

_____

_____

_____

_____

_____

_____

_____

_____

This week notice how your body has delivered and thank her for her service.

Week 11

ENJOY BEING IN YOUR BODY

You know how your body can feel miserable when exposed to allergens and get crampy at regular twenty-eight-day intervals and feel lousy because of everyday bugs and globe-threatening viruses? It's the worst, right?

But at other times she can also feel pretty fantastic.

Some of us were taught (by people we're going to generously assume had the very best of intentions) that it shouldn't feel *too good* to be in our bodies. Some of us learned that we should avoid delicious tasty treats. And steer clear of the devil's rock and roll music. We were trained to be suspicious about anything that made us feel *too* good. You didn't wanna feel too good, that's for sure.

And because a lot of us swallowed the idea that experiencing pleasure was probably the road to damnation, some of us rejected it without ever consulting the One who designed these bodies to experience pleasure in the first place. So let's take a beat and pause to rethink that whole business.

NOODLE ON THIS: What are the ways in which God created human bodies to enjoy pleasure? Where do you notice the generosity of the Creator in the original design? (Just go ahead and get all your thirteen-year-old-boy thoughts out on the table, and then you'll have room to be a little more nuanced about laughter and tickles and sunshine and Ben and Jerry's Half-Baked and the sound of any Stevie Wonder song ever recorded.)

_____

_____

_____

_____

_____

_____

Now, what are the ways that you most enjoy your body? What are the particular choices you make to receive pleasure?

_____

_____

_____

_____

_____

_____

Boots on the Ground (Marching Orders)

This week decide to enjoy being in your body by embracing one practice you've neglected. (Walk in the sunshine over lunch hour? Chew grape bubble gum? Something else?) Specifically, how will it look?

_____

_____

_____

_____

_____

_____

_____

_____

_____

_____

_____

_____

_____

This week enjoy being in your body.

Week 12

SPEAK WHAT IS MOST TRUE ABOUT BODIES— YOURS AND OTHERS

Let me share a tale of two girls. (Boy, I wish I could offer this with a catchy theme song, like the one for *Gilligan's Island* or *Beverly Hillbillies*. Feel free to imagine a catchy tune.)

One little girl grew up with a mama who had drunk the Kool-Aid and believed the lie that her body would never measure up. So she'd make comments about her "muffin top" overflowing out of her skinny-ish jeans. She'd grump about having bad hair days. She'd refuse to leave the house without full makeup. She'd make cracks about her flat chest. And she'd take thirty-nine selfies before posting one of them on the Gram. So, obviously, she was normal.

But the other little girl grew up with a mama who'd decided that, despite the shouty voice of the culture around her, her imperfect body was just right. This girl heard her mother when she prayed before meals thank God for mac and cheese that tastes delicious. She watched her mother look in the mirror and smile at what she saw. The girl heard her mother praise her own thick, strong legs, as well as her daughter's. And she'd compliment other women who were complete strangers on a bright smile, or even on her fierce energy. I do not have to tell you, smart reader, that the second girl grew up to believe that her body was good.

When you speak what is most true about bodies, that they are entirely acceptable as they are, you communicate to other women and girls that their bodies are *just right.*

NOODLE ON THIS: Who are the women you've seen who seem to be entirely pleased with their bodies exactly as they are? And how did or do they communicate this?

_____

_____

_____

_____

_____

_____

_____

And what about you? On a scale of speaking good about your own body and talking trash about it, what do other women and girls hear from your lips?

_____

_____

_____

_____

_____

Boots on the Ground (Marching Orders)

This week purpose to speak what is most true about bodies to another woman. You can marvel at what her body can do, or you can announce the marvel of how your own body functions. Specifically this week, how will this sound?

_____

_____

_____

_____

This week speak what is most true about bodies—yours and others.

Week 13

EMBRACE FREEDOM
IN YOUR BODY

For decades, there was this old gal who skateboarded at Venice Beach in Southern California. Liz Bevington wore bedazzled sweatshirts that proclaimed she was "Skate Mama." This white-haired old gal roller-skated, skateboarded, and even zipped through parking lots on a board with a freakin' *sail*. As a woman who gave zero effs about others' opinions of her, or how they thought old people should behave, Liz Bevington was *free* in her body.

A lot of us who are new-ish to being strong in our bodies are still figuring out what freedom looks like. Well, sis, it looks like what Jesus called life that really is life.

We experience freedom in our bodies when we throw caution to the wind and get stinky sweaty before a PTA meeting because our kid challenged us to a footrace. We experience freedom when we parade through the mall in striped rainbow yoga pants because, despite their inability to hide thigh-jiggle, they just make us *happy*. We experience freedom in our bodies when we scream and jump up and down when we win an antique Cher CD at drag queen bingo.

Freedom looks like letting our bodies do what they were made to do—sweat, jiggle, scream, jump—with utter disregard for the opinions of others.

NOODLE ON THIS: What are the ways that you are still "stuck" when it comes to your body? (For example, refusing carolers at the door if you're not in full makeup. Instead of your fabulous Converse All-Stars, wearing heels because they make your legs look good. You get the idea.)

_____

_____

_____

_____

_____

_____

_____

_____

_____

Sometimes, without even realizing it, we can be bullied by the opinions of others. What would freedom look like if you ignored the opinions of others? Would you stop at a red light on your morning walk to dance to the Jackson 5? Would you eat a delicious apple fritter from Sheetz if you didn't care about men's irrelevant opinions about your bulges?

Describe how you would be free in your body if you cared not a whit about what others thought of you.

_____

_____

_____

_____

_____

_____

_____

_____

_____

_____

_____

_____

_____

_____

Boots on the Ground (Marching Orders)

This week establish one initiative to practice being free in your body. What's your gut telling you? And, specifically, how will it look?

_____

_____

_____

_____

_____

_____

_____

_____

_____

_____

_____

_____

_____

_____

This week embrace freedom in your body.

What I Need:

I DESERVE
GOODNESS

Week 14

AGREE THAT YOU DESERVE GOODNESS

Here's a wily little crazy-maker: when we were children, we believed that we deserved what we got. If there wasn't a mature loving other letting us know that we deserved goodness, we naturally believed we got what we deserved.

If a parent abandoned us, we naturally believed we deserved to be left. If one of our caregivers harmed us—physically or emotionally—we assumed we didn't deserve to be protected. If we saw a friend's parent offering warmth, affection, hugs, and understanding that we didn't receive at home, we deduced we weren't *worthy* of being nurtured.

It sucks, doesn't it?

I would like to sky-write this with environmentally safe airplane smoke and shout it in both your ears and tattoo it on your face: *you deserve goodness!* (Sorry I had to be so aggressive, but it's that important.) You are God's beloved daughter, and you deserve to be protected, nurtured, and loved. You *deserve* goodness.

NOODLE ON THIS: Often, we can look at someone else—a girlfriend, a sweet wittle squishy baby, a woman who has suffered, our daughter—and we know in our deep places that *she deserves goodness.* We do. It's obvious. So I want you to hold in your heart someone who deserved and deserves goodness: girlhood *you.* I want you to sit face-to-face with your girl self, and notice all the protection, nurture, and love that girl needs and justly deserves.

Now write down all the good that you believe she deserves. (If you're horrible at this exercise, invite Jesus to sit beside you and help.)

_____

_____

_____

_____

_____

_____

_____

Boots on the Ground (Marching Orders)

This week I want you to look in the mirror every morning and evening and announce, "I deserve goodness." If it feels awkward, I don't care. Do this every day until you *mean* it. To get you started, write the words here:

_____

_____

_____

_____

_____

_____

_____

_____

_____

_____

_____

_____

_____

This week agree that you deserve goodness.

Week 15

ASSURE ANOTHER WOMAN THAT SHE DESERVES GOODNESS

Even though we have more sophisticated emotional resources when we're grown than we did when we were girls, the enemy still hisses to our hearts, "You got what you deserved." (If you simply have no time for a spiritual being who is bent on wreaking evil and destruction, you might also think of this voice in your head as "the voice that lies.")

When you fail to get the promotion, you might be tempted to believe that you got what you deserved.

When your friend betrays you.

When your husband cheats.

A little voice whispers that you got what you deserve.

And guess what? Other women suspect the same when they're treated like garbage. Even the mighty, powerful women you know and admire may look at the crap in their lives and quietly believe that they deserve no more than they've gotten.

This week, assure another woman that she deserves goodness. If she received a crappy diagnosis, if she can't pay her rent, if her husband left, if she suffers from depression, let her know that she *deserves* so much more than she's gotten.

NOODLE ON THIS: Who are the women in your orbit who've gotten a raw deal?

_____

_____

_____

_____

_____

_____

_____

_____

What are the good things you see in these women and their lives?

Write down a list of affirmations for the specific things you value and find amazing in them.

Boots on the Ground (Marching Orders)

This week practice community and solidarity with those woman you've been thinking of who suffered. Plan a girls' night, and spend some time glorying in all your quirks and how you've been made. Celebrate each other, laugh together, and affirm each other. Declare your list of affirmations over them, and write down the things they speak over you as you together rewrite your learned narratives.

_____

_____

_____

_____

_____

_____

_____

_____

_____

_____

This week assure another woman that she deserves goodness.

Week 16

PRACTICE FIERCE
SELF-COMPASSION

Have you ever experienced a delicious community of people who believe that you deserve goodness and everyone else does too? If you have that now, hang on with both hands and never let go. These are men and women who would never reap the benefits of your losses or keep you low so they can remain high. This is the partner or spouse or friend group or church or work environment that cheers you on, celebrates your successes, pushes you toward new wins, cherishes your health. They offer a fierce compassion that says, "You deserve goodness, and so does everybody else."

If you feel a little bit naughty for even considering this possibility, believe that *it is for you*! And that is why I am officially charging you to begin practicing fierce self-compassion. Today. Now. This very second. Fierce self-compassion says unequivocally, "I deserve goodness, and so does everybody else."

The same women who can boldly affirm the second part too often waffle about the first one. They're the ones who aren't convinced they deserve the job, the home, the life partner, the child . . . you name it! Beloved, as a representative of "everybody else," I am imploring you to let this truth seep down into your deep places: *you deserve goodness.*

NOODLE ON THIS: What is the circumstance in your life, today, where it's hardest for you to believe that you deserve good things?

Write a bit about why you are slow to believe you deserve good and where that might come from.

_____

_____

_____

_____

_____

_____

Now that you've named the place where you're not really convinced that you deserve good things, I want you to use your imagination and describe a reality in which you receive the good that (today) you're not quite convinced you deserve. (This is just for you, so don't hold back.)

_____

_____

_____

_____

_____

_____

Boots on the Ground (Marching Orders)

This week practice self-compassion by fighting to believe you deserve goodness in that one area where it feels most unlikely. Name that area.

_____

_____

_____

_____

_____

_____

This week practice fierce self-compassion.

Week 17

REFUSE TO SABOTAGE
YOURSELF

My girlfriend has a kid who finds a way to tank his birthday every single year. I mean, this kid has never once enjoyed his own birthday party. He'll get irrationally mad and grump in a corner. Or he'll pick a fight with a sibling. He'll "accidentally" dump his *Frozen 2* birthday cake on the floor. Or he'll be extremely weepy, as if the whole world is against him. But the only one who's against him is . . . *him*. Crazy kids! Am I right?

Because grown-ass women like you and me, we would *never*. We'd never sabotage a perfectly good celebration being thrown in our honor. We'd never blow up a good relationship because we're certain they're going to leave us, but we'll show them by leaving first. We'd never.

Except we do. And we're not loony toons, either. We didn't create this nonsense out of thin air. No, there was something painful in our history that still keeps us from *allowing* goodness. If your experience didn't teach you that you were deserving of good things, you may keep sabotaging the potential good that comes your way.

Until now. Sister, refuse to play this whacky game.

NOODLE ON THIS: As you think about your parents, your dating relationships, your friendships, your marriage, and other significant relationships, what are the ways in which you've accidentally or purposefully sabotaged them?

_____

_____

_____

_____

_____

_____

Whatever situation you chose, I now want you to imagine what it looks like for that relationship to thrive, to grow, to flourish. What affirmation do you need to own so that you no longer sabotage yourself? (Example: "The next time a great guy takes an interest in me, I'm going to notice my anxiety but not let it be the boss of me.")

Write an affirmation to help you weather the next good thing you'll be tempted to disrupt.

_____

_____

_____

_____

_____

_____

Boots on the Ground (Marching Orders)

This week repeat that affirmation until your insides are saturated with it. Specifically, how or when will you do this?

_____

_____

_____

_____

_____

_____

This week refuse to sabotage yourself.

63

Week 18

ASSIGN LESS WEIGHT
TO CRITICISM

Back in the 1980s there was an inspirational book written for aging women called *When I Am Old I Shall Wear Purple*. The big idea was that when we're old, we should ignore the opinions of others and just decide to wear and do and say whatever the hell we want. If she wrote it today, I'm pretty sure it would be given the same title as Kevin Hart's COVID-time Netflix comedy special: *Zero F**ks Given*. (To no one's surprise, I fell in love with the entire premise of his show before I ever watched it.) At the ripe old age of forty-one, Kevin Hart had decided that because of his advanced age, the opinions of others mean *nothing* to him. Thus, the giving of zero effs.

Daily, many of us let the opinions of others dictate what we wear. What we do. What we say. And, I suspect you've already learned this from your own experience, being bossed around by what we think others think—while wildly common—is a bunch of horse poop. It is death dealing.

Beloved, do not wait until you're ninety-seven years old to wear purple! If you're a wee babe, don't even wait until forty-one to entirely disregard what others think of you. *Trust me when I tell you that it feels frickin' fantastic.* No one (except me) is going to force this down your throat either; it's a choice you have to make for yourself. And I can assure you that you will *not* regret it.

NOODLE ON THIS: I have a sneaking suspicion that even the most audacious, badass babes among us have some area in which the opinions of others have the potential to crush us (#thatnastyAmazonreviewIshouldnthaveread).

Identify and then list the area or areas in which you're prone to being bullied by the opinions of others.

_____

_____

_____

_____

_____

_____

What would it look like for you to go full purple and decide today that you will remove the shackles and live free?

What safe, healthy choices would you make (or not) if you ignored the criticism (real or imagined) of others?

_____

_____

_____

_____

_____

Boots on the Ground (Marching Orders)

Take your first step into the freedom of ignoring the irrelevant opinions of others. What is one thing you will do this week that you've missed out on because you feared criticism? Specifically, how will this look?

_____

_____

_____

_____

This week assign less weight to criticism.

What I Need:

I NEED
SOME HELP

Week 19

NOTICE AND TAKE PRIDE
IN ALL YOU ACCOMPLISH

Did I mention how women do all the things? We spin the plates, pay the bills, sign the forms, do the work, fix the problems, manage the people, organize the world. And we do it all while menstruating, *and* pushing a grocery cart, *and* tele-conferencing in to work from the vitamin aisle of the grocery store. (It really is the quietest aisle. You're welcome.)

So let's just pause here and notice all the shiz you get done *every day*. I mean, you're kind of amazing. And I want you to own that and take pride in it.

Of course, I recognize the Sisyphean mountain I'm climbing by asking you to take a healthy pride in your accomplishments. Many of us were taught that pride is a sin. And that it goes before a fall. And that it's okay to be proud of others but in no world should we be proud of ourselves. I feel like this might be a vocabulary situation, because I can see how unhealthy pride is destined to lead to a stumble or even a trip.

But healthy pride is different. You have the right to be proud of all you do. If you're not, if you never pause to notice and appreciate all you've done, you're missing out on the satisfaction you've earned and deserve.

NOODLE ON THIS: Look over the last seven days, noticing and recording all you accomplished. (Don't be shy, girl. I saw that sweet note you sent to a teacher. And the pot of chili you made. And the errand you ran for a neighbor. And all the other things. Be *thorough* about this!)

_____

_____

_____

_____

_____

_____

_____

_____

_____

_____

Boots on the Ground (Marching Orders)

This week leave this list where you can see it. Snap a picture with your phone or keep your book flopped open on the counter so you can peek at it. From the list on the previous page, what's the accomplishment, large or miniscule, of which you're most proud?

_____

_____

_____

_____

_____

_____

_____

_____

_____

_____

_____

_____

_____

This week notice and take pride in all you accomplish.

Week 20

IDENTIFY SITUATIONS
THAT WOULD BENEFIT
FROM OUTSIDE SUPPORT

I believe I mentioned that I barely survived parenting my children through early childhood. And you may recall my near miss wasn't like a gentle decline into illness by which I narrowly escaped death. It was more like a running-a-Mack-truck-into-a-brick-wall-at-ninety-miles-per-hour sort of situation. Talking to my mom on the phone one day, between tears-pouring-down-my-face belly sobs, I basically vomited out all the loneliness, resentment, and weariness I'd been silently carrying like the noble martyr I was.

I needed help, and it had never once occurred to me to ask for it.

Maybe you've been there. If you've never been trapped at home with the mayhem that five littles create on the regular,

I suspect you have your own version of "Why would I ask for help when I asked for this and I want the world to think I'm killing it?" Maybe it's a project at your job that keeps you awake at night. Or maybe you live with someone who has an addiction and your sweet, patient, loving presence hasn't yet magically changed the situation. Or you might be caring for a special someone with the kind of big, big needs that can threaten to crush one lone caregiver.

I wish I could tell you that a light bulb came on and I asked for help like a healthy, mature person. Although that didn't happen, and my desperation was only accidentally exposed, I am 100 percent sure that your life will be better, and *you* will be better, if you pause to notice where you need help today.

NOODLE ON THIS: As you survey your life today—possibly with a partner, or as a parent, or as a grown-ish woman who has a family of origin, as an employee, as a caregiver, as someone who may own a car or a home or other stuff that breaks—what are the situations that you're not quite managing well?

_____

_____

_____

_____

_____

_____

_____

As you notice the people and responsibilities and stuff that require more of you than you have to give, identify the one that feels the most overwhelming. What is it that you most need?

_____

_____

_____

_____

_____

_____

_____

_____

_____

_____

_____

_____

_____

Boots on the Ground (Marching Orders)

This week take your first baby step to get help for the situation that feels crushing. Specifically, how will it look?

_____

_____

_____

_____

_____

_____

_____

_____

_____

_____

_____

_____

_____

This week identify situations that would benefit from outside support.

Week 21

NOTICE THE PEOPLE
WHO CAN HELP

Those of us who juggle all the balls and do all the things—and do them *amazingly* I might add—can be tempted to think there is probably no one else on the planet who can do the things. I mean, when there are Styrofoam diorama balls to be purchased, and preschool pickup lines to pollute the planet, and leaky sinks, and cats with diarrhea, and twenty-five classroom birthday cupcakes to be baked (because, for the love of carbs, it couldn't be an even twenty-four), we can be pretty convinced that we are the only ones who could possibly do the things.

"Wait, what? There are oompa loompas behind the bakery counter at the grocery store who bake delicious confections that are available for purchase?"

Mind blown.

This week, as you're treading water, notice the people who can help. If you have a life partner, start there. This is a human with a vested interest in keeping you afloat. If you're able and willing to spend dollars, consider hiring babysitters and grocery deliverers and plumbers. If your situation is work related, talk to your boss. If money is tight, notice the helpers in waiting who want nothing more than to see you healthy: a parent, a sibling, a friend, a neighbor. I promise you there is someone in your life who wants to take over for a few hours so you can go eat three Cinnabons at the mall. This week, notice the people who can help.

NOODLE ON THIS: As you think about the situation you named last week that feels overwhelming, who are the people who can help? (Don't be shy. List everyone who might be useful. In any way.)

_____

_____

_____

_____

_____

Apparently there's this thing now where the people who *could* help turn out *not* to be mind readers. (Now we both know.)

From the list above, identify the right helper.

Helper: _____

How I'll contact the helper (text, call, or email): _____

When I'll contact the helper: _____

Boots on the Ground (Marching Orders)

It's time to get the help you need and deserve! Right now put a reminder on your calendar to contact the helper you've designated above. (Note: Make it at least seven days from today. Because next week you're going to learn the secrets of the *good ask*.) After the ask, write these words below: I did it! I'm stronger and better because I asked!

_____

_____

_____

_____

_____

This week notice the people who can help.

Week 22

ASK WELL

W hen you ask for help, I want you to think it through and *ask well*. Specifically, I want you to ask in a way that makes it easy for a helper to say *yes*. You've identified a situation in your life that needs help. You've noticed who can help. Now I want you to *ask well*. The best ask is one that's *SMART*. So let's workshop this baby.

S: Specific

Think through exactly what it is you need so that you are offering a clear ask.

M: Meaningful

Help the ask-ee understand why you're asking by sharing what it means to you.

A: Action oriented

Ask for something specific to be done. Helpers will be grateful for the clarity.

R: Real

The request you're making should meet an authentic need you have, not one you've concocted to garner attention or create drama.

T: Time-bound

Eliminate all vagueness and be specific about when you need the request to be met.

Now, write out the thoughtful ask you're going to share, loosely using these prompts:

This is what I need and this is exactly how you can help me. **Specific**

This is how I'm overwhelmed. **Meaningful**

This is how I've reached my limits. **Meaningful**

This is where I dream of going. **Meaningful**

I need you to do this. **Action oriented**

This is the real need I have. **Real**

I need you to do this by this day. **Time-bound**

_____

_____

_____

_____

_____

When you ask SMART, you make it easy for a helper to say *yes*.

Boots on the Ground (Marching Orders)

This week choose one (or a couple!) of these asks and reach out to some friends and family for help. Notice how asking more intentionally changes things for both you and your loved ones. How do you picture continuing this practice the next time you find yourself in need of help? What will it look like to make the ask before you're completely overwhelmed?

_____

_____

_____

_____

_____

_____

_____

_____

_____

This week ask well.

What I Need:

I NEED MORE

CONNECTION

Week 23

EXTEND HOSPITALITY TO THOSE WHO MAY BE LONELY

Over the years I've been gifted with the stories of women like you, I've heard a common thread: *I want to be more connected and less lonely.* Whether you're a CEO working eighteen-hour days or a round-the-clock work-at-home caregiver, whether you're single or married, whether your family immigrated here fifteen years ago or had first-class tickets on the *Mayflower*, whether you're a recent college grad or are only months from retirement, it's very possible you feel lonely. (If you think that woman whose life is so wildly different from yours couldn't possibly be lonely, think again.)

If you have rich relationships or if you feel desperately lonely, the key to banishing loneliness is in your hand. (Did you see that coming?! Not everyone does.) Today, you have the power to create safe spaces for others to be seen and loved and known and celebrated.

- Invite a friend to coffee.
- Host a family that includes a teen with a disability for dinner.
- Plan a neighborhood potluck.
- Take a plate of cookies to a mom on your kids' soccer team who's learning English.
- Send a text to let someone know you are thinking of them today.

When you decide to extend hospitality and welcome and love and belonging to others, when you take your eyes off your own loneliness, you bless and you are #blessed.

NOODLE ON THIS: Who are those in your orbit—at church, school, work, neighborhood—who may be in need of relationship? Brainstorm below, and don't omit any name or face that passes through your brain. This exercise obligates you to nothing; you're just making a robust list of folks who come to mind.

_____

_____

_____

_____

_____

Of the folks who came to mind, who is one person who might be feeling lonely and might welcome time with you, with you and your family, or with you and another friend?

Boots on the Ground (Marching Orders)

This week invite the person you identified above to share time. If Martha Stewart hospitality terrifies you, keep it super simple. Specifically, how will you share time together?

_____

_____

_____

_____

_____

_____

_____

_____

_____

This week extend hospitality to those who may be lonely.

CONNECT WITH SOMEONE WHO UNDERSTANDS YOUR UNIQUE SEASON AND CHALLENGES

Lara is a busy working mom of three littles, and she's friends with Tamika, a mom to a five-year-old son. Since her recent divorce, Tamika and her ex-husband have been sharing joint fifty-fifty custody of their son. When Tamika and Lara met up at a park recently, Tamika mentioned that after the park she needed to get her son to his dad's house.

Lara replied, "I wish I got to have a break! You can go to a movie, get a pedicure—"

Tamika's heart stung, hearing those words from her friend. She didn't want a pedicure. She wanted to be with her son in an intact family, and Lara's trite dismissal made her feel even more lonely.

As you consider the fruitful connections in your life, reach out to someone who understands the unique challenges of the season you're in. Maybe she'll be a recent widower, like you. Maybe she's single and hoping for marriage, like you. Maybe she's a person who shares your culture. Maybe she's building her own business, like you. Connect with someone who understands the gifts and challenges with which you live.

NOODLE ON THIS: What are the particularities of your life in this unique season? (Notice age, gender, family, work, faith, health, disability, race, culture, and so forth.)

_____

_____

_____

_____

_____

And as you notice these parts of yourself, who is a person or people that you might reach out to so that you can connect with someone who "gets" that about you?

_____

_____

_____

_____

Boots on the Ground (Marching Orders)

This week reach out to one person who can relate to
the part of you that needs extra care and attention.
Specifically, what will you ask of this person?

_____

_____

_____

_____

_____

_____

_____

_____

_____

_____

_____

_____

This week connect with someone who understands
your unique season and challenges.

Week 25

MAKE ONE NEW
GENUINE CONNECTION

R emember how when you were a kid you played kick the can with other kids in the neighborhood? And remember how when you were in high school you had friends at church, or on the volleyball team, or in the thespians club? And then remember how when you were in college you ate in the cafeteria and drank endless Diet Cokes with the girls in your dorm? For a lot of us, there have been seasons in life that were more *ripe* for relationship than the one we're in today.

You don't need to go out and join a sorority—and, frankly, if you're over twenty-two this is ill-advised—but there are plenty of opportunities for you to make new personal connections with others. And I'm not suggesting that you need to make twenty new BFFs. Just open yourself to receiving *one new friend*.

Here are some places where you might connect with someone new:

☐ Neighborhood
☐ Kids' schools
☐ Workplace
☐ Gym
☐ Book club
☐ Activist groups
☐ Running club
☐ Support groups
☐ Bible studies
☐ Playgroups
☐ Professional networks
☐ Volunteer groups
☐ Motorcycle clubs
☐ Special interest spaces (knitting circles, writing groups, cooking clubs, dog lovers)

And, just like you were hunting for a man on a dating app (which you also might be doing), I want to encourage you to be open to the possibility that your new friend might come in unlikely packaging. (If you're lucky, she will.) Maybe she lives at the group home in your neighborhood. Maybe she checks a different box on the census form than you do, but you both share a weird obsession with TikTok pranksters. Or maybe she'll be a few decades older than you. Open your heart and take the steps to make one new genuine connection.

When you browse through those possible places to connect, which one feels like it might have your name on it?

_____

NOODLE ON THIS: It's possible that the person with whom you might connect is already in your orbit. Close your eyes and think about the women who've made you say, "She'd be great to know, but—" Maybe you were too busy. Maybe you assumed she had all the friends she needed.

List the ones who you've been interested in getting to know but haven't taken steps to make it happen.

_____

_____

_____

_____

_____

_____

Boots on the Ground (Marching Orders)

This week take your first step toward a new place to meet friends or toward a person who's been on your heart. Specifically, what will you do?

_____

_____

_____

_____

_____

_____

_____

_____

_____

_____

_____

_____

_____

This week make one new genuine connection.

Week 26

BECOME AN INTEGRAL PART OF SOMETHING GREATER THAN YOURSELF

A girlfriend of mine used to be a real joiner. You probably know the type. (You may *be* the type.) Maria joined all the things, and led all the things, and she would work herself to the bone, lose sleep, and feel crushed by the weight of it all. In order to survive, she'd have to move to a new town where she'd feel okay for a minute, but then she'd join new things. Eventually she got healthy and learned how to say no. (Yay, Maria! You did it!)

Maria, divorced, had just become an empty-nester when the global pandemic rolled around, and a few months in she noticed she was feeling aimless and lonely. While it's great that she had boundaries of steel, she'd also been missing out on the connection that comes from being *engaged* with something bigger than ourselves. When a friend of hers released a book about grief that Maria knew would help a lot of people, she volunteered to host an online event for the launch. That opportunity gave her the chance to connect with others by being a part of something bigger than herself.

This week I want you to think about those places where you are an integral part of something that's bigger than you. Maybe you organize likeminded folks who are fired up about the same social cause you care about. Or perhaps you volunteer one Saturday each month at Habitat for Humanity. Or maybe you've struck up a new friendship through a ministry serving alongside people with disabilities.

If you don't feel connected to something that's bigger than you, I want you to begin thinking about what might have your name on it.

NOODLE ON THIS: What are opportunities to connect that meet another's need?

_____

_____

_____

_____

_____

NOODLE ON THIS: What are opportunities to connect that enliven you?

_____

_____

_____

_____

Since I've already pegged you as a pretty smart cookie, you've probably figured this out: the big win is to connect to something greater than yourself that meets a need and enlivens you.

Boots on the Ground (Marching Orders)

What opportunity do you see to connect with something bigger than yourself that checks both of those boxes—meeting a need and enlivening you?

_____

_____

_____

This week become an integral part of something greater than yourself.

What I Want:

I WANT
THIS DREAM

Week 27

GRANT YOURSELF
PERMISSION TO DREAM

When you have dared to want, to imagine, to dream of what you might do with your life, have you heard another annoying wet blanket voice attempting to smother your dream? This interfering voice protests, "Yes, but we really *are* called to sacrifice—" or "I mean, have some dreams, sure, but don't really give your all in pursuing them—" This wearisome internal voice, which sows fear and brings judgment, has zero investment in you doing the thing you were created to do. It hisses accusations like "greedy," "ambitious," and "selfish."

I think you and I both know what that voice can do with her opinion.

Sister, this world needs for you to dream. We need you to do the creating, inventing, and contributing that only you can do. And when you finally decide to own the dream that's been percolating inside of you—*forever*—the world will flourish because of it. Whether you've felt stifled because of gender limitations, poverty, oppression, white supremacy, or simply by that voice that's bullied you from the inside, now is the time to silence her and go after the dream inside of you waiting to be unleashed.

I want you to review your life, year by year, and remember the dream you held in your heart in each of those seasons. Did you dream of dancing? Writing? Painting? Cooking? Speaking? Selling? Though you may not have had the insight or tools to know exactly how your dreams would unfold, the dreams you had as a girl, or a teen, or an ambitious young adult are *clues* to what you might dare to dream today.

NOODLE ON THIS: No matter how unrealistic someone told you they might be, list the different dreams you've had for your life over the decades. No dream is too big or too small.

_____

_____

_____

_____

_____

_____

As you notice the dreams you recalled above, do you notice any that make your heart beat a little faster today? And, specifically, is there a different expression of the dream that feels more right today? For example, maybe when you were twelve you imagined owning a cupcake bakery and today you dream of catering parties.

Note below the updated dream you're holding in your heart.

_____

_____

_____

_____

Boots on the Ground (Marching Orders)

This week repeat the affirmation, "I choose to dream." Write those four words below—maybe in big fat bubble letters?—as your first announcement.

BRING YOUR DREAM
INTO THE LIGHT

A girlfriend of mine is a creative. She's pretty much just a whole bunch of creativity with some skin on. I mean, there is no end to all the ideas she has for books, and businesses, and social action, and paintings, and catchy commercial jingles. And one day she's in a bookstore and sees a book someone has written that really seems like they ripped off the idea for the book she planned to write. So when she dropped a choice curse word in the Christian Living aisle of Barnes & Noble, her life partner thoughtlessly mused, "There's nothing new under the sun." That's when dragon steam started coming out of my friend's ears and eyeballs and mouth and nose. (All the head holes.)

What she knew, to which her partner seemed oblivious, was that no one else can do what she could do in the way that she could do it. ("Nothing new," my a$$.) It's true. No one has done your work already, because they couldn't possibly. There is an empty void right where your talent belongs. If you're hiding your dream under a bushel, we need you. We need you to bring your dream into the light of day. Like, *yesterday*.

Okay, so I'm hoping and assuming that you've begun to notice the dream that's in your heart. Maybe it's one that was seeded when you were a girl. Or maybe you had an experience along the journey that has birthed this possibility inside you. This week I want you to do two things to bring this dream—that only you can realize!—into the light.

1. **Share the dream with one person.**

   Not everyone is prepared to receive your dream. Share it with someone you trust and who believes in you.

2. **Take your first baby step to live the dream.**

   You do not need to hire an attorney to copyright your big idea. Today just take a wee little baby step in the right direction.

NOODLE ON THIS: As you consider the dream in your heart, who is the right person with whom you can share your dream? (This person is trustworthy and believes in you.)

NOODLE ON THIS: What is one baby step you could take toward pursuing your dream this week? Make a phone call? Purchase a tool? Other? (Note: We're going to be talking action items that will get you where you're going during the next few weeks!)

_____

_____

_____

Boots on the Ground (Marching Orders)

This week take one step toward realizing your dream. Specifically, what will you do?

_____

_____

_____

_____

_____

_____

_____

This week bring your dream into the light.

Week 29

DECIDE THAT YOU ARE NOT ASKING FOR PERMISSION

B ecause human beings are literally wired for lives of meaning, occasionally your ambition is going to rub up against someone else's dormant desire, and that feels bad to them. Your forward movement reminds them of their own stagnation, so an easy shot is to say you are a big dummy, a try-hard, conceited, doomed to fail.

Here's a fun party game: If these Negative Nellies get at you, I am predicting that it's because they're sitting in camp chairs on the sidelines. And the Positive Patties who are cheering you on are likely the folks who are running their own race. Feel free to email me if I'm wrong. But I really don't think I am. About this.

Decide in advance that you are not asking for permission. You may appropriately be open to feedback but not dismissal. This is a huge part of becoming an integrated woman. You have agency over your own life, and it is not up for grabs. Obviously, be willing to receive good counsel or strategic advice or useful suggestions as to your path forward, but that does not include handing your dream over for rejection. Protect your dream in its undeveloped infant stage like it's your job. Because it is.

NOODLE ON THIS: The ones who are going to cheer you on are those who are busy living large. They're pursuing their dreams and they're thrilled to see you pursue yours.

Who are the people in your orbit who you see flourishing because they're pursuing their dreams?

_____

_____

_____

_____

_____

_____

The Negative Nellies who have the most potential to threaten your dream are the ones who voice the words of your *own internal critic*: "Who do you think you are?" "You're not equipped." "You'll likely fail."

Go ahead, just get them out of your system right now by naming your own objections and then countering them with what is more true.

The critic says: _____

But truth says: _____

The critic says: _____

But truth says: _____

The critic says: _____

But truth says: _____

The critic says: _____

But truth says: _____

The critic says: _____

But truth says: _____

Boots on the Ground (Marching Orders)

This week cling to a mantra that reminds you that you don't need the permission of others. (See "But truth says___" on the previous page!) Specifically, what are you choosing to believe this week about the likelihood of your success?

_____

_____

_____

_____

_____

_____

_____

_____

_____

_____

_____

This week decide you are not asking for permission.

Week 30

LEARN THE ROPES

Apparently, 81 percent of Americans believe they should write a book.[1] Yet common sense dictates that 81 percent of Americans should probably *not* write a book. Now I'm no dream crusher, but . . . *common sense*. Still, we know that some portion of the 81 percent are going to sit down at their laptops this year, open up a blank document, save it under the file name "My Book," and start banging away at the ol' keyboard. Do I want these brand-new author babies to pursue their dreams? Of course I do. But I also believe that, whatever our dream, we need to commit ourselves to learning the ropes. Whether the dream you hold in your heart is to publish a book, open a restaurant, practice medicine, throw clay pots, or work on a farm, you need to learn how that particular job or task is done.

I'm sorry to perseverate on this book-writing business, but . . . *81 percent*. (I see you, reader, with that book in your

1. https://www.nytimes.com/2002/09/28/opinion/think-you-have-a-book-in
-you-think-again.html.

heart that's begging to be born.) You learn the ropes when you invest time and money into attending a conference for writers. You learn the ropes when you join a group of other writers and critique one another's work. You learn the ropes when you read and analyze the books other writers have written.

If you're serious about going after your dream, commit yourself to learning the ropes.

NOODLE ON THIS: Notice the dream that's in your heart and consider how you can learn the ropes. Who are the people *I know* who are already succeeding at doing this thing?

_____

_____

_____

Who are the well-known experts who are already doing this thing?

_____

_____

_____

What are the books and blogs and podcasts that equip people who are doing this thing?

_____

_____

_____

What are the training opportunities or internships for people who are doing this thing?

_____

_____

_____

Where are the peer groups of people supporting one another as they do this thing?

_____

_____

_____

What are the other opportunities I can access to learn the ropes related to doing this thing?

_____

_____

_____

Boots on the Ground (Marching Orders)

This week contact one person you know who's doing this thing. Don't demand a lot of their time, but do ask, "What is the most important thing I can do to learn the ropes?" When they answer, write their advice here:

_____

_____

_____

_____

_____

_____

_____

_____

_____

_____

_____

_____

This week learn the ropes.

Week 31

DO THE HARD
WORK REQUIRED

Reader friend, I love your dreams. I love your wild, amazing ideas. I love how you are wired. I love the stuff that fires your engine. I love how your eyes light up and you start talking too fast.

You've owned your dream, which is the first step. (Can you hear me clapping, and cheering, and cat-calling?!) And now it's time for the part that is known as hard work: research, exposure, brave requests, strategic emails, new classes, workshops, purchasing materials, up-front financial investments, joining professional groups, calendar reorganizing, jettisoning some prior commitments, observation trips, a million YouTube tutorials, market research, skill development, important conversations, information compilation.

That hard work isn't just a means to the end. It is a precious asset in and of itself. Those hours, all the conversations, the learning, the setbacks, the stuff before results—this builds something strong in you you'll need for the long haul. You find out what you're made of when no one is watching, much less applauding.

Do. The. Hard. Work.

Maybe there's a part of this dream building that really scares you. Maybe you've dreamed of creating a nonprofit, but you don't have a lot of confidence in your ability to be a strong leader. Or maybe you've imagined establishing a thriving business that serves your customers, but you've convinced yourself that you don't have a business mind. Great news: you can learn!

The parts of dream building that feel the scariest are likely the parts of the dream building that are going to *feel* like work. As you think about what needs to be done to achieve your dream, notice which work will come easy, which will feel like work, and which will feel grueling.

NOODLE ON THIS: As you think about what needs to be accomplished, note which tasks will come easily, which simply require work, and which feel very difficult.

This "Work" Is Life-Giving for Me

_____

_____

_____

_____

_____

_____

_____

This "Work" Needs to Get Done, So I Rise and Grind

_____

_____

_____

_____

_____

_____

This "Work" Is Death-Dealing for Me

_____

_____

_____

_____

_____

_____

Boots on the Ground (Marching Orders)

This week take three steps toward accomplishing your dream by doing one task that's easy, one that requires midgrade exertion, and one that feels pretty difficult. Specifically, how will it look?

Easy: _____

Harder: _____

Most Difficult: _____

This week do the hard work required.

What I Want:

I WANT
TO CHOOSE
MY YESES

Week 32

CHOOSE THE RIGHT YES

Adult life is chock-full of choices. It is a war between a myriad shoulds, shouldn'ts, won'ts, don't want tos, wish I coulds, I guess I wills, and do I have tos. The average woman is presented with one thousand choices for every one hundred slots. Waiting in the wings to accompany each reluctant yes or apologetic no is resentment, exhaustion, unproductiveness, and guilt.

Making reluctant choices that don't reflect our actual desires is a major breach; we have to work hard on integration here. We must steer our own ships or risk capsizing under too many waves or becoming lost at sea.

I want you to be very intentional about your yeses. When chosen carefully, a well-placed *yes* can be the best decision of your life. The right yeses can completely, utterly, fantastically change your trajectory. And the wrong yeses? Well, they can suck the life right out of you. They can hog up those one hundred slots so that when the possibility that is the *rightest* for you comes along, there's no room for your good, right yes.

You can see where this is going, right? Choosing the right yes depends on you having the courage, all along the journey, to say the right no.

If you're like most women who've ever lived on this planet, it's likely that you've said some yeses you now regret. Maybe you were reluctant, said yes out of obligation, and were miserable because of it. Or maybe you really thought you were offering a good yes, only to later discover that your decision should have been a no. You said yes to hosting the gala. You said yes to planting and tending a rose garden in front of the church. You said yes to mentoring that really sweet, young gal. Live and learn.

NOODLE ON THIS: You've lived, and now it's time to learn from your living. Over the years, what have been the yeses you regret? Little ones and big whoppers.

_____

_____

_____

_____

_____

_____

_____

And . . . what have been your very best yeses ever?!

_____

_____

_____

_____

_____

Boots on the Ground (Marching Orders)

This week write these words on a note and stick it to
your bathroom mirror: "I am choosing the right yeses."
Write it here to practice:

_____

_____

_____

_____

_____

_____

This week choose the right yes.

Week 33

EMBRACE SIMPLE YESES THAT MOVE YOU TOWARD YOUR GOAL

You have a dream; you can see the goal; and you are on fire about getting there. YES!

It turns out that the journey from having the dream to reaching the goal involves a whole bunch of steps. So with your eyes on the prize, the job is to determine and choose the yeses that will get you to the goal. What do you want? Where do you want to go? What simple yeses will move you toward that goal?

For example, if you've set your mind on building physical endurance, one of the simple yeses you might choose is scheduling a run every morning before you start the day. It's a simple yes that moves you toward your goal. If you're starting a nonprofit that serves kids fighting cancer, make one phone call a day to invite potential donors to join you. It's a simple yes that moves you toward your goal. If you want to do a live podcast tour (#guilty), then research the cost of tour buses. It's a simple yes that moves you toward your goal. These yeses are like dominoes; just tip that first one.

You've already said the big yes to the big dream. The mission. The goal. The prize. And to get there, your mission is to embrace the simple yeses, one by one.

NOODLE ON THIS: Because you've got lots you want to accomplish, notice what you want to do, who you want to be, and where you're headed. Name a simple yes that can help get you there.

This is the dream I want to achieve:

_____

_____

And this is a simple yes I can embrace to achieve it:

_____

This is a goal I have for my body:

_____

_____

And this is a simple yes I can embrace to achieve it:

_____

This is a goal I have for a relationship:

_____

_____

And this is a simple yes I can embrace to achieve it:

_____

This is a skill I'd like to learn/master:

_____

_____

And this is a simple yes I can embrace to achieve it:

_____

Boots on the Ground (Marching Orders)

Notice your simple yeses listed above and choose one that you'll embrace this week. Specifically, how will it look?

_____

_____

_____

_____

_____

_____

_____

_____

_____

_____

_____

_____

This week embrace simple yeses that move you toward your goal.

Week 34

REVOKE YOUR
PROBLEMATIC YESES

Remember that time that woman asked you to do that thing? And you know how you said yes, sort of reluctantly? And then you kind of resented her for having the nerve to even ask you? Then you got madder and madder, at her and at yourself and at the world? And you even got furious at your husband for not being the person who said yes? (But let's keep it real: If he had answered the phone and been asked to do the thing, he would not have said yes. And this makes you even more livid.) Sister, you're not alone.

A lot of women have a difficult time saying no, especially if we think someone's feelings may be at stake. But this temptation of ours actually isn't genetically determined. In fact, Dr. Kathryn Lively wrote that our yeses are a socially learned coping mechanism that can be unlearned. (Didn't Dr. Kathryn Lively just elbow her way into a coveted spot in your pantheon of self-help goddesses, right between Brené and Oprah?)

We are tempted to offer problematic yeses in lieu of saying a difficult *no*.

Because we tell ourselves that saying yes was the only choice we could have made, and saying yes was obviously the *morally* superior choice, and that only a monster would say no, we too often convince ourselves that we've offered a good yes. And since we do have such a vested interest in not letting others down—even that pushy gal who asked us to do the thing we don't even really care for anyway—we convince ourselves that our yes was a good one. Except it wasn't.

NOODLE ON THIS: Do any of the yeses below resonate with ones you've offered? Check each box that feels familiar and jot down a note beside it—a name, a task, etc.—to remind you of your own terrible, horrible, no good, very bad yes.

- I said yes when I wanted to say no.
- I said yes sincerely, but now life has shifted.
- I said yes naively, and this isn't working.
- I said yes because I felt bad.
- I said yes because I felt obligated.
- I said yes to spare someone's feelings.
- I said yes gladly, but it has run its course.

- I said yes, and now it is time to pass the reins.
- I said yes, but I need to create margin now for something else.

I am delighted to be the one to inform you that you are entitled to revoke your problematic yeses! And, if you're serious about accomplishing that thing only you can do, you're sort of *obliged* to revoke them. And although you don't owe anyone a reason for pulling out, the solution is actually tucked right there in the original problem:

- Life has shifted.
- This isn't working.
- It has run its course.
- It's time to pass the reins.
- I need to create margin now for something else.

Boots on the Ground (Marching Orders)

This week notice one problematic yes—that you offered for the wrong reasons—and let the right person know that you can no longer continue. Specifically, how will this look?

_____

_____

_____

_____

_____

_____

_____

_____

_____

_____

_____

_____

_____

_____

_____

_____

_____

_____

_____

_____

_____

This week revoke your problematic yeses.

Week 35

HAVE CONFIDENCE
IN YOUR NO

Tell me if you've seen this crazy math before:

Saying "Yes" = GOOD
Saying "No" = BAD

While I certainly understand some of the reasons this crooked math has come to be, and I even confess to using this absurd calculator myself in my weaker moments, let's just agree once and for all that this twisty thinking is keeping a lot of us from what we were made to do and who we were made to be. And we are *not about that life.*

Just as there can be bad yeses, there are also fabulous life-giving, necessary nos. As the saying goes, the greatest enemy of the best is the good. Here is where your yeses need the nos as solid partners. Each of us has a limited amount of time and energy, and it will reach its capacity. Choosing new yeses means a few new nos too. We subtract so we can add. #moremath #sorrynotsorry

If you're already knee-deep in a commitment that you know is not right for you, your first good no is going to be what we mastered last week: revoking a problematic yes. If a commitment has lost its original joy, or is something better outsourced, or has run its course, or has outlived its usefulness, or just needs to go because it needs to go, revoke your previous ill-advised yes.

I also want to get you hyped up so that you're prepared to offer a no and really stand by it the next time the opportunity presents itself. Can you take responsibility for getting one hundred new donors to our fundraiser next week? No. Will you take on this additional project at work? No. Can you lead this new ministry at church? No. (Obviously, I added that last one to remind you that while some nos will feel great, others will feel horrible, even if you know for sure that a no is the best decision for you and your people. It can be really hard.)

When you've offered your no with integrity, you can have confidence in your no.

NOODLE ON THIS: Let's review your track record. When have you said no to others' requests? And what did you learn, about yourself or others, by saying no?

_____

_____

_____

_____

_____

_____

Boots on the Ground (Marching Orders)

Because sometimes requests can take us off guard, I want you to be ready by having your next no on the tip of your tongue. Write _no_ below—multiple times to get in practice.

_____

_____

_____

_____

_____

_____

_____

This week have confidence in your no.

What I Believe:

I BELIEVE IN
SPIRITUAL
CURIOSITY

Week 36

GIVE YOURSELF
PERMISSION TO EVOLVE

During the Scopes Monkey Trial of 1925, when the State of Tennessee accused high school teacher John T. Scopes of teaching human evolution, a nutty dichotomy between science and religion was fueled. In that moment the religious pitted the *Bible* against science. Fast forward to 2020, when yard signs across America during the COVID-19 pandemic read, "I believe in science." (Also a beautiful, if accidental, homage to Nacho Libre's buddy Esqueleto.) I'm just gonna say what we're all thinking: *the bar has been set pretty low.*

And yet, because the particular spiritual culture that shaped many of us operates in absolutes, natural curiosity is viewed with hostility. In this subculture, when you follow all the rules, when you hit all the marks, and when you stay inside the lines, you're rewarded. But when you step outside those lines—when you question, when you push, when you challenge—you risk getting booted out of the club. (Or so I hear. This is what they're saying.)

Beloved, this wasn't God's big idea. In fact, in the Jewish tradition, spiritual curiosity isn't just tolerated, it's *celebrated*. A serious person of faith is willing to evolve. When you allow yourself to *evolve*, when you make room for your heart and mind to explore what is, you grow. So keep asking those hard spiritual questions that make the most religious among us uncomfortable. God can handle them. You can too.

NOODLE ON THIS: What are one or two beliefs that you once held, or now hold, that you've been told shouldn't be questioned? (Investigating these has been deemed taboo by the religious.)

_____

_____

And here's some space to write a quick note to the Almighty, offering your heartfelt queries to One who cares.

_____

_____

_____

_____

_____

_____

Beloved, this is just a beginning. Continue to ask questions, read, study, and get into fabulously sticky conversations with people who see things differently than you do. Keep going.

Boots on the Ground (Marching Orders)

This week pursue one person who has ideas and opinions that differ from what you've been told. Let them know you want to learn and grow, and then be a great listener. Specifically, how will it look?

_____

_____

_____

_____

_____

_____

This week give yourself permission to evolve.

Week 37

HAVE THE COURAGE
TO BE HONEST

In ancient caveman and cavewoman days, burly manly men would go out on hunting trips and throw their spears at tasty wild animals and women would stay home, tend the garden, and keep all the babies alive. I'm not endorsing this, as I know a few women who love to toss a spear, I'm just reporting it. Many men have a vision that's *macular*, keeping their eyes targeted on accomplishing the one thing, the one goal. And many women have a vision that's more *peripheral*, noticing and tending to the needs of those around them. Again, just reporting.

Because many women value our relationships and connections, we can be reluctant to do anything to disrupt them. Specifically, if we have questions or doubts bubbling up inside us, some of us have learned to tamp them down so that we don't disrupt our relationships by rocking the boat. We fear excommunication, family outrage, community rejection, and even being wrong. And those fears keep us silent.

While I wish I could tell you that those concerns are unfounded, they're not. The cost of being honest can be high. And because exercising brave honesty can create ripples, I understand the temptation to bury your questions and zip your lip.

But, sister, the cost of silence is pretty high too. When you refuse to be honest, you either lose something of yourself or you fail to grow into the authentic woman you were created to be. I know it can feel scary (I really do), but I can also tell you that gathering your courage to be honest is worth it.

NOODLE ON THIS: Maybe there's been a little something bubbling up inside you. Maybe a truth you never went looking for has taken up residence inside you and now it's time to speak it. Or maybe there's a question in your gut that you were once willing to ignore but are now noticing the price you've been paying for your silence.

What is inside you, about which it's time to be honest?

_____

_____

_____

_____

_____

_____

When you're practicing living with integrity and take the brave risk to be honest, you kind of know who is going to be freaked out by it. As you think about externalizing the truth that's been inside you, that's not the person to start with.

With what safe person or people can you be honest? (Note: They don't need to agree with you; they just need to be working with mature adult emotional resources.)

_____

_____

_____

_____

_____

_____

_____

_____

Boots on the Ground (Marching Orders)

This week choose one safe person with whom you can share honestly about what's inside you. Specifically, how will it look?

_____

_____

_____

_____

_____

_____

_____

_____

_____

_____

_____

_____

_____

This week have the courage to be honest.

Week 38

CARE ENOUGH TO ASK HARD
SPIRITUAL QUESTIONS

Perhaps you've met one of those know-it-all types, who can just drop a single Bible citation bomb in the comments as proof that you are absolutely wrong and she is obviously so wildly right. (I hope you're *not* that gal, but if you are, stick with me.)

Something about that aggressive and abrasive certainty doesn't ring true, does it? Something feels a little bit off about having a tweetable sound-bite answer for every last blessed thing. It would be great if it were all that easy, but it's not. It's just not.

Virtually every spiritual person has his or her beliefs challenged during their lifetime. Not only is this nothing to be ashamed of, but it's actually the road, or the path, into which the Bible invites us. Scripture calls this good way *wisdom* and *maturity* and *growth*. (If you maybe thought that asking hard spiritual questions was called *heresy* and *backsliding* and *unfaithfulness*, you've gotten bad intel. Sorry, Charlie.) A person asking hard questions of her faith system cares, and that means something. Asking hard questions doesn't indicate an anemic faith but the opposite! Contrary to the shady practices of the religious who squeeze their eyes shut to ambiguity and contradictions within the Bible and thoughtful queries, a faith that asks hard questions is the most robust kind of faith.

Care enough to ask hard spiritual questions.

NOODLE ON THIS: You know how, when you brainstorm, you just vomit out everything inside you and worry about cleaning it all up later? Yeah, that's what I want you to do now. Using *zero* internal filters, I want you to brainstorm all the spiritual questions living inside you. If you don't know where to start, open the Bible and begin in Genesis with the population of the planet. Enough said.

Record all your hard spiritual questions. (If you need more paper, pull out an old journal or notebook. Or a five-hundred-page three-ring binder.)

_____

_____

_____

_____

_____

_____

Boots on the Ground (Marching Orders)

This week stay open to asking hard spiritual questions.
When you decide to open yourself to them, they'll
come! Specifically, where will you jot them down?

_____

_____

_____

_____

_____

_____

_____

_____

_____

_____

This week care enough to ask hard spiritual questions.

Week 39

DISCERN WHAT IS ETERNAL
AND WHAT IS CONTEXTUAL

I love me some Bible. I really do. And different believers have different ways of understanding which parts of the Bible are timeless truths—#love, #truth, #justice—and which are contextual, with more relevance for the culture and day in which they were written and less relevance today. For instance, the prohibition against wearing wool and linen fabrics in one garment. (I wouldn't hate hearing *Queer Eye*'s Tan France's opinions on this.) If you read the Bible while wearing your thinking cap, which I highly recommend, you'll notice that, while many of the truths and laws in the sacred text are timeless, others are contextual. There's a lot we can hold loosely.

I have no interest in prescribing for you what is contextual and what is eternal. I can, however, tell you what I know for sure:

- Jesus is good.
- He is love and love alone.
- He is for us, never against us.
- He fixed the broken space between us and God.
- He was the greatest living human (he slayed at humanity) and lives to intercede eternally for us.

I believe that in Jesus is life. I'll never believe anything else, anything less. Those are my non-negotiables. They're eternal. When everything else in the world and in my life is shaky, these are what remain solid.

I'm so proud of you for being open to the idea of open-ness. And because there's always going to be some gray area with the potential to make us anxious inside, I encourage you to discern what is eternal and cling to the essential.

NOODLE ON THIS: Throughout the history of the Christian church, theologians and scholars and brainiacs and common folk have sought to discern what is essential to the faith and what is peripheral.

Spend some time this week and jot down what you believe to be essential and eternal.

_____

_____

_____

_____

_____

_____

_____

_____

Boots on the Ground (Marching Orders)

This week cling to the one rock-solid conviction of yours that is most essential. Specifically, what is it?

_____

_____

_____

_____

_____

_____

_____

This week discern what is eternal and what is contextual.

What I Believe:

I BELIEVE IN
THIS CAUSE

Week 40

LISTEN TO WHAT IS
BURSTING IN YOUR CHEST

A girlfriend of mine who was raised in the whitest of all affluent suburbs has a fiery passion for racial justice. It bursts in her chest. She cared about it as a teen. During college she visited South Africa to learn about reconciliation efforts there. She hustles in her workplace for justice, and every day she wears a Black Lives Matter T-shirt. Every day. I'm not even kidding. Right now she's wearing one. It's a whole collection: "BLM to this Mom." "Every day BLM." "BLM to Jesus." "BLM in Houston." There's no end to these shirts. (When anyone asks her why, she just points to her knockers and answers, "Prime real estate here. So I'm using it for good.")

I mention her particular passion because I want you to pay attention to the problem or injustice or challenge or inequity that matters most to you. Maybe you care deeply about a particular group of people. Or animals. Or the environment.

When you notice this particular wrong, you get fired up to make it right.

Friend, we need you to own the passion that burns inside you. What is that thing that is bursting in your chest? Listen to it. Give it energy, give it life. Circle up with the coconspirators who have the same internal thumping and go make some good trouble. Put your stake in the ground: "I care about this. I believe in the possibility of wholeness here. I am all in. I would march for this." No hiding or shirking. No prioritizing criticism or the opinions of others. Just beautiful compassion while doing work that matters for those who deserve goodness, same as anyone.

NOODLE ON THIS: One of the ways we recognize the unique passion we've been given is to gaze back over our lives and pay attention to the moments when we were fired up, or stepped out, or advocated, or lobbied, or marched, or cried.

What causes have you championed with your time, your energy, your dollars?

_____

_____

_____

_____

_____

_____

And if you had to name the passion you hold closest to the center of your heart today, what would it be?

_____

_____

_____

_____

Boots on the Ground (Marching Orders)

This week, choose to own the passion within you about which you cannot be silent. To honor it, embrace one tangible action with your time or your money. What will that be?

_____

_____

_____

_____

This week listen to what is bursting in your chest.

Week 41

BE FOR OTHERS

In his book *Mere Christianity*, C. S. Lewis wrote, "Do not imagine that if you meet a really humble man he will be what most people call 'humble' nowadays: he will not be a sort of greasy, smarmy person, who is always telling you that, of course, he is nobody. Probably all you will think about him is that he seemed a cheerful, intelligent chap who took a real interest in what you said to him."

I can only guess that being greasy and smarmy were problematic in 1952. If you're able to ignore the grease and smarm, the gendered pronouns, and the fact that no one in this century is even striving to be a humble human, he gets at something really important: this "chap who took a real interest in what you said to him" is a person who is *for* others.

I'll bet you know someone like this. The Sunday school teacher at church who is genuinely interested in your child. The neighbor who mows your unkempt lawn just because. The mentor who checks in on you for no reason at all. People who are for others are people we want to know and be known by.

Be someone who is for others. It is good for others, obviously. And it's actually really good for you. Being for others takes our eyes off of our own petty problems and enlivens us as we care for others. And it is good for the *world*.

With strangers and family and friends, in big grandiose ways and teeny tiny ways, be a person who is *for* others.

NOODLE ON THIS: Who are the saints you know—in your life or out in the world—who are living lives that are for others? (In the good way. Obv. Not the codependent way.)

_____

_____

_____

_____

Actually, that little parenthetical caveat, above, is worth paying attention to.

How are you being for others in a way that enriches your life?

Healthy ways I'm being for others:

_____

_____

_____

_____

_____

_____

Boots on the Ground (Marching Orders)

This week how can you be like that "humble guy" who takes a real interest in others? Specifically, how will it look?

_____

_____

_____

_____

_____

_____

_____

This week be for others.

REFUSE TO SPEAK FOR

THE "VOICELESS"

I have an announcement to make: there's a whole big lie going around about a group of people who *do not exist*! It's kind of like one of those internet hoaxes that too many dummies believe, although this one got rolling way before the internet. The people group in question are "the voiceless." (If you're one of those suckers who is hell-bent on believing that these imaginary people exist, why don't you locate one and ask them. I swear on a stack of Target gift cards, if you can find a person with vocal chords, whether or not they are physically functioning, and suggest that person is voiceless, he or she will find a really clear way to communicate to you how wrong you are.)

Over the years, some of the very best people, who likely had the best intentions, have decided to speak up for these imaginary "voiceless" ones. What they're failing to see is that the allegedly voiceless have only been marginalized and bullied into voiceless-ness because those of us who've centered ourselves have just been so hoggy, and loud, and fervent, and privileged.

The reality is that the person we've silenced has a voice. Not only does she have thoughts and words, she also likely has *solutions*. She has agency. She has power. I sincerely hope this is not coming as a surprise to you, but if it is, I understand. The wily lie has really made the rounds for a number of years.

If, like me, you've been privileged enough to have been handed the microphone, can you imagine what it might look like to hand it off to someone else? If the person who handed it to you really wants you to use it, this will be an opportunity for him or her to grow. And you can facilitate that. I mean, really get creative about this business of sharing the mic with those whose voices *we've just been ignoring.*

NOODLE ON THIS: You likely have opportunities to amplify the voices of the voice-ful who've just been shushed by mic-hogs for too long. At work. At church. In the community. On the soccer field. In all the places.

What unique opportunities have you been afforded by your particular circumstances—Teacher? Coach? Mom? Employee? Boss?

Blogger? Podcaster? Ministry leader? Mary Kay saleswoman?—
that you can utilize to amplify voices the world desperately
needs to hear?

_____

_____

_____

_____

_____

_____

_____

_____

_____

Okay, you noodled on the situational opportunities to
which you have access. Now I want you to shift your focus
away from yourself, close your eyes, and search for the faces
of those whose voices need to be heard. They might be folks
you know. They might be more public.

Who is one special someone whose voice you can amplify?

_____

Boots on the Ground (Marching Orders)

This week, on your social media channels, share an article, or podcast, or book, or video by someone from a group that's been historically marginalized. Specifically, how will it look?

_____

_____

_____

_____

_____

_____

_____

_____

_____

_____

_____

_____

_____

This week refuse to speak for the "voiceless."

Week 43

PAUSE TO LISTEN AND LEARN
FROM THOSE WHO KNOW

When I say that we should refuse to speak for the voiceless, it doesn't mean go home, make yourself a margarita, kick up your feet, and binge-watch *Housewives of Atlanta*. There is work to be done! And when your heart is burning for that worthy cause, you may recall that I am also advising you not to go all bull-in-a-china-shop about it. This is why I am delighted to inform you that there is a happy medium between bull-mayhem and checking-out housewife-foolery. It is called settle-down-so-you-can-listen-and-learn.

Because the pain of others does trigger something primal in us, we're tempted to grab the steering wheel without a clue in the world where we should be headed. And yet faithful advocacy requires a stage of listening and learning. No matter how wild with passion you are over an issue or people group or need, someone else is already on the ground with more knowledge, experience, and best practices. Someone else is already on the ground having long been on the receiving end of that injustice. Someone else is already on the ground with hard-won lessons, a mobilized community, and an accurate perception of the big picture. Helping poorly can be worse than not helping at all.

The best advocates are humble about learning.

NOODLE ON THIS: What is the issue or people group or need your heart is burning for today?

_____

_____

One of the spaces where I've had the gift of learning from those who know is Latasha Morrison's Be the Bridge community on Facebook. That space was my classroom and the community my teachers. (And, honestly, I think the "don't comment or post for three months" rule should be implemented worldwide for us newbies.)

Maybe you don't yet know where the spaces are and who the experts are where you can listen and learn. But you know that whole six-degrees-of-separation business? Chances are good that you know someone who knows someone who can guide you in the right direction.

Who can direct you to the best sources to listen and learn?

_____

_____

_____

_____

_____

_____

Boots on the Ground (Marching Orders)

This week identify and pause to enjoy one opportunity to listen and learn. Specifically, how will it look?

_____

_____

_____

_____

_____

_____

This week pause to listen and learn from those who know.

Week 44

CHAMPION YOUR CAUSE
IN WORD AND IN DEED

Y ou've identified the passion that's burning inside you. *Hooray! I'm shaking my pompoms for you, girl!* Because we were designed to feel the emotions of one another, your *heart* is where your fierce passion is conceived. But it was never meant to stay there. What is growing in you, the conviction that's been gestating for nine months or nine years, is meant to be born! In fact, the world needs it to be born and articulated and expressed and championed. Eventually we need to put our boots on the ground by championing our cause out loud in word and in deed.

Go ahead and start with your words. (Just don't end with them.) Maybe you'll share your convictions on the internet with your people. That's a good place to start. You know what place is a little trickier? Your family's Thanksgiving dinner table with Grampa Joe and Uncle Ted. (Yeah, I went there.

This is why God created holiday comfort foods like stuffing and pecan pie.) Have a conversation with your brother-in-law, and your neighbor who displays *those* political yard signs, and the old but surprisingly feisty loudmouth lady at church. (Pot calling kettle black, you say? Yeah . . . I hear it now.)

Using our words is a place to start advocacy, but it can't end there. We need to put some capital behind what we stand for. Maybe it's *literal* dollars. Maybe you support the fantastic organization doing grassroots work that's changing lives. Or maybe the capital you invest is your actual body, marching for something in which you believe. Or maybe you wield your social capital to make an even bigger difference. You invite folks who know and trust you to join you in the street, at the hospital, or in the prison.

If your fiery passion has somehow gotten stalled in your heart, today is the day to use your voice and lace up your marchin' boots.

NOODLE ON THIS: How have you already acted on the passion in your heart with your voice and your body and your dollars and your energy?

_____

_____

_____

_____

_____

_____

_____

_____

NOODLE ON THIS: As you consider your physical voice, and the written word, and your actual body, and the money you control, and the energy inside you, what are other possible opportunities into which you're being invited to spark change?

_____

_____

_____

_____

_____

_____

_____

_____

_____

Boots on the Ground (Marching Orders)

This week how will you externalize the passion inside you—with your voice and your body—in a new way? Specifically, how will it look?

_____

_____

_____

_____

_____

_____

_____

_____

_____

_____

_____

_____

_____

_____

This week champion your cause in word and in deed.

How I Connect:

I WANT TO CONNECT WITH HONESTY

Week 45

CHOOSE TO BE TRUSTWORTHY, MATURE, AND AUTHENTIC

Most of us consider ourselves to be people who highly value truth-telling. It's other people who lie, right? Actually, we love truth-telling except when we don't, we practice it except when we don't, we require it except when we don't. It is okay to admit this, because it is ubiquitous to humanity. Admitting this can be liberating. It also makes it trickier to silently judge the people in our lives who lie. We do it because, at some level, it serves us. We do it to be agreeable, so others will like us. We do it to feel better about ourselves. We do it to smooth out awkward social interactions. And sometimes we do it because we simply lack the courage to tell the truth.

But just because we all do it, doesn't mean that it is

serving anyone. (Though knowing and offering the right answer to "Do these jeans make my butt look too big?" or "Do these jeans make my butt look too small?" may serve to preserve a friendship.) And, in fact, we can likely gauge the health of our relationships by noticing where our interactions land on the scale between teeny misleading, polite, nicety kinds of lies and calculating deceptive, big, whopper lies. Specifically, chronically dishonest people generally have relationships marked by distrust, turmoil, and shallow connections. (I know someone like this, and I suspect you do too.)

On the other hand, chronic honesty tends to arc with trustworthiness, mature conflict resolution, and authenticity—key building blocks of healthy connections. As you purpose to connect with honesty, commit yourself to being trustworthy. Being mature. Being authentic. There will likely be a bit of a learning curve that may feel awkward and bumpy and unfamiliar, but as you keep choosing honesty, your relationships will benefit.

NOODLE ON THIS: List three situations in which you fudged on the truth, a little or a lot.

_____

_____

_____

_____

_____

_____

And as you reconsider these situations, imagine more trustworthy, mature, and authentic ways to handle the situations,
noting them below.

_____

_____

_____

_____

_____

_____

_____

_____

_____

_____

Boots on the Ground (Marching Orders)

This week notice one situation in which you are tempted to offer words that aren't the whole truth, or couched in passive aggression, and purpose to do it differently. When you do, note it here:

_____

_____

_____

_____

_____

_____

_____

_____

_____

_____

_____

_____

This week choose to be trustworthy, mature, and authentic.

Week 46

PRACTICE MINDFULNESS
BY NOTICING WHAT IS

A number of years ago a friend's husband was sitting up in bed reading a book by a woman named Byron Katie called *Loving What Is*. When he explained the big idea of Katie's book—choosing to notice what is, without getting all rattled by it—my friend thought it was the most inane, stupid, dumb-dumb thing she'd ever heard. But a few months later she happened to watch Byron Katie on *Oprah* discussing the book. And then she thought it was the most insightful, genius, life-changing idea she's ever heard in the history of the world.

This business of *noticing what is* is a form of mindfulness. Mindfulness is a nonjudgmental, zoomed-out, from-a-narrator's-perspective description of simply what *is*. It includes a neutral stance toward yourself and the actual moment at hand. It is particularly useful for those of us who can easily get bossed around by our feelings. (When I say "us,"

I obviously mean "me.") I am someone who can be dominated by My Feelings. I didn't choose it, but it turns out that this is the way I'm wired.

So when it comes to practicing radical honesty with others, it can feel overwhelming in the moment with another person. The anxiety of the unknown, what the person might think about me, and what the consequences might be if I tell the truth can be *a lot*. And that's why I choose to practice mindfulness by noticing what is. I pause, take a breath, and notice what's going on without any judgment before I speak or react.

Try it. It's magical. Or if you've really got your panties in a wad about some minor offense you've suffered, that feels very large as you obesess over it for days, you can use the same technique. Try practicing mindfulness like that, on your own, first. Notice how liberating it can be, and then attempt it in face-to-face situations.

I want you to have the opportunity to practice this game-changing technique for living honestly. And without losing your mind. So think of a recent occurrence that really stuck in your craw. Maybe your mom was forty minutes late meeting you for lunch on Saturday. For absolutely no good reason. Or maybe you've been stuck thinking about why your ex has never ever owned up to what he did to you. You get the idea.

Describe the thing that's been eating at you:

_____

_____

Now that you've named what's bugging you, I want you to detach from it. Maybe see yourself lifting up and out of your body, floating like hummingbird, looking down at what happened like you are a casual observer with no skin in the game. Now you can practice mindfulness by noticing what is—your mom being late to lunch—and detach from that the meaning you'd assigned to it. ("She's so selfish." "She doesn't think of anyone but herself." "If she cared about me, she'd get her poop in a group and be on time." Etc.)

Below, jot down the *meaning* you assigned to the event ("He is a nar-cissist." "He is broken." "He never loved me.") and choose to let it go.

_____

_____

_____

_____

Use a journal to practice mindfulness as an exercise to help you do it in real time.

Boots on the Ground (Marching Orders)

This week pull out an old journal (one that doesn't feel fresh because you already wrote on the first three pages) and practice mindfulness. Specifically, when will you practice, and what event will you return to?

_____

_____

_____

_____

_____

_____

_____

_____

_____

_____

_____

_____

This week practice mindfulness by noticing what is.

Week 47

PRIORITIZE DIRECT COMMUNICATION

"What will she think if I'm honest about what I'm really thinking?"

Whether it's a relationship with your boss, a coworker, a friend, a spouse, a pastor, or someone else in your world, it can feel scary to speak clearly and honestly. So, instead, we bitch about her to others. Or we tell him what we think he wants to hear. Or we completely avoid dealing with the thing that is begging to be dealt with. We don't mean to be jerks, but all of it feels easier in the moment than prioritizing direct communication.

Let's say you have a friend who maybe acts like a bossy know-it-all when you're together. She has lots of other fine qualities, but this is one you keep experiencing. And, let's be honest, it doesn't feel good. You can choose to ignore it, but if you do that, you suffer and your relationship suffers. And eventually you're just going to stop doing things with her because you don't want to feel icky. And maybe you'd rather bail than have a hard conversation because the thought of it makes you feel anxious and overwhelmed.

But you're an honest badass woman with grown-woman skills, so one day you gather your courage and say, "Hey, I need to let you know that, lately, when we hang out, I don't feel great about our time. In fact, I feel small after we're together. When you correct me frequently and laugh when I don't know something you know, it feels crappy to me." Now, your friend might respond all different kinds of ways, but what you've done is give the relationship a chance to change and flourish. Even though it can feel scary, gather your courage and prioritize direct communication.

NOODLE ON THIS: Is there a situation or relationship, right now, that would benefit from you communicating directly? What is it? Who is it?

_____

_____

_____

_____

I want you to imagine what this situation is going to look like when you put on your big-girl panties and handle your business by communicating directly.

Below, workshop some good language you can use when you maturely engage with this person.

_____

_____

_____

_____

_____

_____

Boots on the Ground (Marching Orders)

This week gather your courage and engage with that person with whom you've not been communicating directly. Specifically, how will it look?

_____

_____

_____

_____

_____

_____

This week prioritize direct communication.

Week 48

REJECT SILENT
COMPLACENCY

As human beings, we naturally fear death. Ladies, do you know why we drop a dime on creams and powders and bleaches and colors and goos to lighten our hair, pink our cheeks, hide our wrinkles, smooth our skin, widen our eyes, plump and shine our lips? We do it all to give the appearance that we are not old, not aging, and, ultimately, not dying. (Want to get up in my grill about this and tell me how super wrong I am? Well, you know who has smooth clear skin, bright round eyes, rosy cheeks, and shiny pink lips? Babies, that's who.)

At a primal level, we fear death. And when we need to pony up and be honest in a relationship, we worry that our honesty will threaten, sever, or destroy the relationship. And so to keep it together, to avoid a rupture (that at some level feels like a little death), we avoid honesty. We keep our big mouths shut. We zip it up. We practice silent complacency.

But here's what no one's talking about: most primary alliances can survive even the most brutal honesty. (Though if there's an nonbrutal way to do it, certainly choose that way.) On the other hand, silent complacency is the kiss of death. Do you see how that whole thing just got flip flopped? Our fear of conflict whispers that the relationship won't survive if we speak up, when in fact staying silent is more likely to kill it! Now you know.

Something inside us tells us that conflict leads to death, but I want you to hear that it can actually lead to life. Practicing honesty and not over-fearing confrontation is the mark of healthy people and their subsequently successful partnerships.

NOODLE ON THIS: Where in your life have you been practicing silent complacency, either intentionally or unintentionally?

_____

_____

_____

_____

_____

Be thoughtful about how you are being called to defeat silent complacency by speaking up.

What is it that you are being called to say in this moment?

_____

_____

_____

_____

_____

_____

Boots on the Ground (Marching Orders)

This week honor a relationship in your life by believing in it enough to end your silent complacency and speak up. Specifically, how will it look?

_____

_____

_____

_____

This week reject silent complacency.

How I Connect:

I WANT TO
CONNECT
WITHOUT
DRAMA

Week 49

STEP AWAY FROM THE RELATIONSHIP DEFINED BY DRAMA

While I confess to enjoying a *lot* of the hogwash my grandpa rejected (#InstaFilters), I actually share his contempt for drama. Wanting to weed it out of my life, I looked at my relationships and environments and asked a few questions that helped me curate the people I've invited deeply into my world. The helpful questions I posed were:

Is this relationship mainly one-sided?

If you're always the listener, always the giver, always the problem solver, you likely feel depleted and not seen. Or maybe the relationship only happens on her terms: when it's convenient, how it's convenient. If so, it's one-sided.

Does this person lie or gossip too much?

If you notice your b.s. radar going off around someone who lies or gossips, don't ignore it. You don't have to put up with being lied to on the regular or listening to a lot of garbage gossip. (It feels awful, because it *is* awful.)

Does this person create constant drama, then expect everyone else to fix it?

If you're cleaning up a friend's ten-thousandth self-imposed crisis, it's possible you're not a friend but an enabler. We get what we tolerate.

This is the "friend" who treats you like garbage. It's the roommate who is never sorry and always right. It's the family member who refuses healthy boundaries. When others are making these choices, you don't owe them your presence, time, and energy. Step away from the relationship defined by drama.

I'm guessing that, as you've been reading, the thought of a special someone has filled your heart.

Right now, what relationship do you suspect may be unhealthy for these reasons? (Tip: Be brave. Is it the guy you met three weeks ago on Hinge? Is it someone who's knit into the fabric of your life? This journal is just for you, so be honest.)

_____

_____

And just in case you have mightily fortified defenses and no one immediately comes to mind, noodle on these questions:

Is there a relationship in my life that is mainly one-sided?

_____

_____

_____

Am I in relationship with a person who lies or gossips too much?

_____

_____

_____

Is there someone who creates constant drama, then expects everyone else to fix it?

_____

_____

Boots on the Ground (Marching Orders)

This week, prayerfully consider one person in your world who may be toxic in these ways. Specifically, what step will you take to step away from them?

_____

_____

_____

_____

_____

_____

_____

_____

_____

_____

_____

_____

This week step away from the relationship defined by drama.

Week 50

SURROUND YOURSELF
WITH HEALTHY FOLKS

You are so super welcome for the three insightful relationship questions last week meant to help you notice people in your life who may not need to be there. But the truth is, you already know the relationships that drain you and the ones that give you life. The ones that drain you are one-sided, involve gossip or lies, and are dripping with drama. Ick. Yuck. Buh-bye. But what about the ones that vivify you, that enhance your flourishing? Let's notice and celebrate those!

I want you to mentally scroll through all your spheres of human interactions and quickly assign your people to these very crude categories. (Be sure to cover home, family members outside of your home, friends, work, school, church, kids' or partner's friends, neighbors, etc.) Don't think too hard, just dish them out like playing cards.

Being with This Person Feels Life-Giving

_____

_____

_____

_____

_____

Being with This Person Is the Normal Mix

_____

_____

_____

_____

_____

Being with This Person Feels Death-Dealing

_____

_____

_____

_____

_____

Based on what I'm discovering, here are some people with whom I choose to surround myself. If we're not getting enough time, I want to be intentional about surrounding myself with these healthy folks:

_____

_____

_____

_____

Boots on the Ground (Marching Orders)

This week take the initiative to get together with one human person who gives you life. Specifically, how will it look?

_____

_____

_____

_____

_____

_____

This week surround yourself with healthy folks.

COMMUNICATE YOUR BOUNDARIES CLEARLY

Were it not for that whole sticky legal issue called *plagiarism*, you know I would have copied and pasted the entire contents of the book *Boundaries* right into *Fierce, Free, and Full of Fire*. Doubling the number of pages, it would have made for one heavy and expensive book, but even if you had to pay double, I think you still would have thanked me. It is *that* good.

What I want you to know about choosing to erect healthy boundaries in your life is that they are about *you*, not the other person. They're not about controlling or changing his or her behavior, although they may have that effect. They are not about punishing someone. They are not mean or selfish or retaliatory. Boundaries might not change anyone else's behavior at all. The only thing they guarantee is what you will or will not do, what you will or will no longer put up with, what you will or will not accommodate. That's it. Boundaries are entirely about you. They are calm, clear words backed up with calm, clear actions:

- If you booty-call me at 11:30 p.m., I won't be picking up the phone.
- If you choose to drink and drive, I will find another way home.
- If you use curse words to demean me when we disagree, I will be happy to finish the conversation when you can be respectful.

When you choose to communicate your boundaries clearly, don't expect the other person to throw you a parade. They are not going to love it, and if they're not a safe, healthy person (duh . . . the whole reason for the boundaries in the first place), it's possible they will lash out by saying mean words to you. Know that it's par for the course. Any way you slice it, you are not in control of their choices or reactions. Only yours.

At this point, I think it's possible you have taken a step away from unhealthy folks in your life and chosen to surround yourself with healthy ones. Get it, girl. But it's not black and white, is it? More often it's pretty gray. And that's where the healthy boundaries come in.

NOODLE ON THIS: As you think about the relationships in your life that are a little unwieldy, which ones could benefit from establishing healthy boundaries?

- _____
- _____
- _____
- _____
- _____
- _____
- _____

And just like the boundaries shared above, how will you calmly and clearly articulate the boundary you are asking of each person?

- _____
- _____
- _____
- _____
- _____
- _____
- _____

Boots on the Ground (Marching Orders)

This week be brave. Choose just one person, above, and share with him or her the healthy boundary you're establishing. Specifically, how will it look and sound?

_____

_____

_____

_____

_____

_____

_____

_____

_____

_____

_____

_____

_____

This week communicate your boundaries clearly.

FINAL
THOUGHT

Week 52

WRITE YOUR OWN

MANIFESTO

This is it. This is the moment you've been waiting for! You've been doing the hard work to become the world's only Glorious You, and I'm so proud of you for that. Take a little bow.

You will build your manifesto of twelve personal statements on the twelve affirmations from *Fierce, Free, and Full of Fire* that we've been exploring here:

I am wired this way.
I am exactly enough.
I am strong in my body.
I deserve goodness.
I need some help.
I need more connection.
I want this dream.

I want to choose my yeses.
I believe in spiritual curiosity.
I believe in this cause.
I want to connect with honesty.
I want to connect without drama.

Sister, week by week, page by page, you've already been doing the hard work of noticing and owning Glorious You. Now it's just time to synthesize all the pieces into a manifesto that can guide you as you continue to become more and more gloriously you. (Is that even *possible*?!) As you return to it in the weeks and months to come, it's going to do two things for you:

1. It's going to remind you of your priorities, commitments, and goals.
2. It's going to alert you if you're tempted to stray from the brave path to becoming your fiercest, freest, and fieriest self.

I'm offering the twelve FF&FoF statements as a template to help you craft your own beautiful manifesto. Some of what you write may be common knowledge, some private, some secret, some brand new. Integration means your inside voice, your outside actions, your thoughts and beliefs, your dreams and hopes—all being in alliance. You are telling the truth.

This is who you are at all times with all people. You aren't pretending or hiding. You decide to be your whole real self, and I can tell you right now, you will not regret this. This is freedom.

I want you to approach this guided by only your heart and mind, but if for some reason you get stuck, consider these hacks:

- Peek at the table of contents and return to the journal pages where you unpacked what each statement meant for you.
- If you're super-duper stuck, you can peek at my manifesto in the appendix of this journal. (I tucked it back there so that it won't distract you if you don't want to look.)

You can start by making a few notes here, before crafting your final manifesto:

I am wired this way.

I am exactly enough.

I am strong in my body.

I deserve goodness.

I need some help.

I need more connection.

I want this dream.

I want to choose my yeses.

I believe in spiritual curiosity.

I believe in this cause.

I want to connect with honesty.

I want to connect without drama.

Okay, sis, it's go time. Depending on how words best flow out of you, grab this journal and gel pen or open up a blank document on your laptop and *get to it*!

You are fierce.
You are free.
You are full of fire.

I am cheering you on in every way, dear sister.

FINAL THOUGHT

JEN'S MANIFESTO

- I am wired as a motivated, high-functioning, introverted Enneagram Three. I love leading but have to work harder on self-assessment and emotions. I have a strong prophetic nature. When I'm healthy, I'm authentic and care deeply for people. When I'm disintegrating, I overvalue success and clamor for approval.

- I take up a large amount of space, because I am jammed with ideas, convictions, and dreams. I like big experiences. I like big feelings and big spaces. I'm comfortable with a large capacity and plan to fill it.

- I want to honor my body as the loyal, strong companion she is. I have been hateful to her for most of my life, and I am determined to love her better.

- I deserve goodness, even in religious spaces where I am an outlier. I am still a good sister and God's kid, and I don't deserve mischaracterization, rejection, and gossip.

- I have learned to ask for help, and thus my life is as well-manned with partners and managers as it ever has been. I feel very supported.

- I am incredibly connected to my friends and family. This is one of the greatest areas of health in my life.
- My dream is to lead millions of women toward lives of great meaning. I care about their souls, their families, their gifts, their churches, and their communities. I also have a side dream of working with food. (Cookbooks, travel writing, cooking show, I don't know! It's a side dream, guys!)
- I have been careless with a few yeses, which created awkward interactions and messy clean-ups for my assistant and team. This is lazy, thoughtless behavior that needs to change. I have two clear nos to give right now that I've held in purgatory with maybes.
- One biblical concept I am curious about right now is the many interpretations of heaven and hell. I'm being challenged by the diverse scholarship around an idea I've only understood one possible way.
- I would march for the eradication of white supremacy, LGBTQ rights and dignity, gun reform, women's safety and equality worldwide, a safe family for every child, and the end of human trafficking.
- I am too indirect a communicator with my family. I want to be honest and present in every moment instead of stuck in the past or rushing to the future. I also need to be more direct with my staff and team. I've not been as good a leader as they need.

- The one place I can still occasionally get sucked into drama is online, and although I've grown here, I always regret biting back or being snarky or joining a pile-on. While not bailing on important discussions and even disagreements, I am opting out of online drama when it is mean and unproductive.